TOO LATE FOR
THE FESTIVAL

TOO LATE FOR
THE FESTIVAL

AN AMERICAN SALARY-WOMAN IN JAPAN

Rhiannon Paine

Academy Chicago Publishers

Published in 1999 by
Academy Chicago Publishers
363 West Erie Street
Chicago, Illinois 60610

I am indebted to Nicholas Bouvier's beautiful *The Japanese Chonicles*
(San Francisco: Mercury House, 1992), for the explanation of Shinto my-
thology.

"In a Station of the Metro" by Ezra Pound, from PERSONAE. Reprinted
by permission of New Directions Publishing Corp.

Grateful acknowledgment is made to Vintage Books for the quotations
from *The Tale of Genji*.

Grateful acknowlegment is made to Columbia University Press for the
quotation from *The Pillow Book of Sei Shōnagon*.

Library of Congress Cataloging-in-Publication Data

Paine, Rhiannon.
    Too late for the festival : an American salary-woman in Japan /
Rhiannon Paine.
     p.   cm.
    ISBN 0-89733-471-X
    1. Women—Japan—Social conditions. 2. Businesswomen—
Japan—Social conditions. 3. Culture shock—Japan. 4. Intercultural
communication—Japan. 5. Hewlett-Packard Company—Officials
and employees. I. Title.
   HQ1762.P35   1999
   305,42'0952—dc21   99-11637
                                      CIP

TO HELEN CLAIRE ROBERTS AND
IN MEMORY OF JAMES DONNE ROBERTS
"THE BEARS WHO WENT OVER THE MOUNTAIN"

• • •

I have not been so fortunate as to know you,
But now I may say how sad it has been to part.
—Murasaki Shikibu, *The Tale of Genji*

A NOTE ON PRONUNCIATION

Japanese is hard to read and write, but easy to pronounce. The consonants are sounded more or less as in English. Vowels are sounded as in Italian.

A   like the a in "ma" or "pa"
E   like the a in "Sadie"
I   like the e in "be"
O   like the o in "okay"
U   like the u in "Sue"

Hence, *Ikeda* is pronounced "ee-kay-dah" and *Muto* is pronounced "moo-toe."

Double vowels, like the two *i*'s in *"subarashii,"* indicate that the sound is held a beat longer. These long vowels are sometimes indicated by doubling, as in *"subarashii,"* and sometimes by a line over the vowel, as in *Kyūshū.*

Foreword

THE BUDDHIST-PRAYER MAN

Whenever I have a sleepless night—and I have lots of them, not being too talented at sleeping—I think of Japan. Here in Healdsburg there's nothing to keep me awake except my thoughts, but in Tokyo there was so much more. The neighborhood dogs used to start barking at bedtime. They were terriers, black and straw-colored, and stunted-looking like the trees in the thin strips of garden around the houses. They couldn't grow big in Tokyo; there wasn't enough room. So they'd bark all night, poor bonsai dogs, and fall asleep at dawn to dream of American spaces: cornfields, orchards, the suntanned hills of California.

Or were those my dreams? It was hard to tell because I wasn't getting much sleep, what with the dogs barking, traffic thundering down the Inokashira Dōri, and the *bōsōzoku* boys snarling their machines through the streets of Nishi Eifuku. *Bōsōzoku* are motorcycle gangs. The boys rev their engines during the wee hours to prove how bad they are, but being Japanese, they try to do this *all at the same time*. After a year or so with the *bōsōzoku*, they junk their black leather gear and get office jobs. Rebellion, Japanese style.

In the autumn of 1986, I started trying to appreciate the *bōsōzoku* boys and also the dogs, the packaged octopus in the Summit supermarket, and the man who drove a loudspeaker truck through my neighborhood on Sunday mornings, playing a Buddhist prayer. I wanted to appreciate them because I knew I'd be leaving Japan soon. But I had been resisting the experience for more than a year and it was too late to give in. I would sit up late at night, longing for California, having fantasies in which the *bōsōzoku* boys lost control of their motorcycles and ran over the bonsai dogs, with consequences fatal to all parties.

In the words of a Japanese proverb, I was *ato no matsuri*—"too late for the festival."

And now I'm home on another sleepless night, and instead of looking out my window at a view that's uniquely Californian—because where else can you see redwood and palm trees in the same glance?—I close my eyes and picture neon signs lit up with *kanji*—willows soaking their branches in the green lake at Inokashira Park—and salary-men sleeping on the last train home from Kichijoji. I smell green tea and cigarette smoke (my nose wrinkles); I see glossy black heads bent over desks. At his terminal with the pink stuffed animal on it, Fingers types like a man on speed. The Imp's laugh rings out. Christine Yamada wishes me "Good morning." Yoz says, *"Ohayō gozaimasu."* Harpo, of course, says nothing. And Miyuki smiles.

I live like a counter-Buddhist, ignoring the present, taking shallow breaths, filling myself with selfish desires. I practice wrong thought, wrong speech, wrong conduct, and wrong means of livelihood.

If you can't stay focused on the present and if the future is, in its annoying way, still in the future, there's only one thing left to do.

I'll just have to dwell on the past.

SPRING

The first sunrise.
There is a cloud
Like a cloud in a picture.
—*Shusai*

One

⚬

ALL SHOOK UP

I woke suddenly in a strange bed. It was ten minutes past midnight by my alarm clock, which was bouncing up and down on the nightstand like a commercial for long-life batteries. But what time really? I counted on my fingers, trying to work out the time difference, and then gave up. In the uncurtained picture window across the room I saw my reflection go wavering across the glass, a ghost with wild dark hair and an O-shaped mouth. The hotel's luggage stand leaned forward, bowing to me, and dropped my big green suitcase on the floor.

I'm a native Californian and no stranger to earthquakes, but this was the first time I'd experienced one from the midsection of a Tokyo skyscraper. Should I get up? Get dressed? Run down twenty-two flights of stairs to get crushed under one of the ship-sized chandeliers in the lobby?

By nature, I'm not a person who springs into action. I'm more of a person who sits around and thinks. It seemed to me that if I was going to die, I might as well die in bed, so I plumped up the pillows and leaned back. I started by wondering if my friends Paul and Tessa Coleman were all right in their apartment in Mitaka. It would serve Paul right, I thought, if I got

11

squashed into human sashimi in the ruins of the Century Hyatt Hotel, and he had to find someone else to document his software. It was his fault I was here.

"Dear Nano," Paul had written to me, five months earlier, "how can I persuade you to come to Japan and work with us as a Foreign Service Employee? How much money do you want? We need you desperately!"

It was the most seductive e-mail message in my experience. I'd been a technical writer at Hewlett-Packard Company for three years and I had certainly been kept busy, but none of my managers had ever confessed to needing me "desperately." Nor had the question "How much money do you want?" been posed nearly as often as I would have liked.

Paul's message continued:

> As you know, Tessa and Duncan and I have been here for a year, working on a special project for Hewlett-Packard Japan, HP's Japanese affiliate. We have a budget for a technical writer for one year, starting in April, 1985. Our SPN group will soon have almost thirty people. They are wonderful, though primarily of the male persuasion. The work should be interesting. . . .

Managers were always telling me that our work was interesting. I always pretended to agree, sensing that an honest response, like "About as interesting as sludge," would detract from my next performance review. But I'd worked with Paul and his wife, Tessa,* for two years before they moved to Japan, and I didn't doubt his sincerity. If he thought that writing software

---

* HP doesn't usually allow a married couple to work together. The Colemans worked for the small start-up company that originated the SPN software, and when HP acquired the company in 1982, it acquired Paul and Tessa as well. Paul's skills and knowledge were crucial to the product line, so he was allowed to go on working with his wife.

for semiconductor manufacturers was interesting, well, he came from another planet, that was all. A planet where, at the moment, large salaries were apparently on offer.

I had just come home to Silicon Valley after a six-month leave of absence from Hewlett-Packard, which I'd spent traveling around Europe on the cheap. My checkbook reflected, with dismal accuracy, the fact that I'd earned no money for months. Visa bills that I couldn't afford to pay had started arriving from Paris cafés and London bookstores. Although relations were still cordial, the friend I was staying with was starting to hint that it would be nice if I had an apartment of my own.

And here was Paul Coleman asking, "How much money do you want?"

I wrote back, "I've just got home from Europe, Paul, remember? I've been traveling for six months and I never want to see a suitcase again unless it's stuffed with money."

"We'll give you a suitcase stuffed with money," Paul responded, explaining the Foreign Service Employee "compensation package." I roughed out a budget and calculated that in one year I could save as much as ten thousand dollars: a fortune. The most I'd ever had before was four thousand dollars. It had taken me five years to save it, and I'd just spent it all on my leave of absence.

So I had assented. I would work for Hewlett-Packard Japan for one year, starting in April, 1985. "My poverty but not my will consents," I wrote to Paul. If you have to give in, you might as well do it with a quotation from Shakespeare.

The alarm clock stopped its manic dance. The Century Hyatt Hotel rocked gently on its heels and then subsided. I slid back under the covers, but I couldn't sleep. I wasn't afraid of aftershocks. I was afraid because I had come to live alone in a foreign country. I had lived in England for five years back in the seventies and I wasn't afraid then, but I didn't see England as foreign. I saw England as a grown-up United States, regal with years and dignity, a bit stodgy perhaps, but full of useful advice for us youngsters. "Wear your wellies in the rain. Speak properly. Don't be impertinent." And Europe, although more foreign than England, wasn't nearly as foreign as Japan. A German woman had stopped me on the street in Freiburg and asked me for directions. She thought I was another German. No one in Tokyo was ever going to take me for Japanese. I was going to stand out, and I don't like standing out. I like to blend in.

For many years I had cherished an image of myself as a Sophisticated World Traveler, a Citizen of the World. I was *not* the stereotypical American abroad, rampaging about in search of New York steak, central heating, and someone who speaks English. I wanted to be a portable person, someone who could make herself at home in any country. Plop me down in Burma or Nigeria or Costa Rica and you'd see how well I could adapt! In no time at all I would learn the language, master the culture, and make loads of wonderful friends.

So here I was in Tokyo, plopped. I was trying to be optimistic, but I had a feeling that my Sophisticated World Traveler image was going to be difficult to maintain in Japanese circumstances. I'd played a lot of roles in my thirty-seven years, some more persuasively than others. Wife of a British Merchant Navy Officer was one of my failures. My ex-husband is a thoroughly good man, but I never mastered the knack of saying, "So, darling, how's your cargo of liquefied ammonia?" as if I gave a damn. I did better as Candidate for M.A. Degree in English Literature at Liverpool University. I got the M.A., after learning how to churn out statements like, "Disbelief did not give rise to disregard; Hardy's inability to give intellectual assent to supernatural phenomena added to rather than detracted from his interest in them."

In the past few years I had learned to write shorter sentences and achieved modest success as a technical writer. Now, though, I was being asked to play not only technical writer, but also American Salary-Woman in Japan.

ALL SHOOK UP 15

Living in England, I had tried hard to be English. I'd worn tweeds, drunk endless cups of tea, adopted an English accent, cultivated reserve, and never talked about money. (This was easy to do since I didn't have any.) I hadn't become English—the accent never fooled anyone but Americans—but I had changed, inside and out. "How do you feel about getting divorced?" my best friend asked me when I moved back to America. I fixed her with the look that English people give you when you ask "impertinent" questions and changed the subject.

If I were to prove similarly susceptible in Japan, I could end up in a Buddhist monastery with all my hair shaved off. Of course, Japan wasn't going to accept me the way that Britain had. Britain had held out her arms and said, Welcome home, I remember your dear grandparents, would you like to see the family albums? Japan had greeted me with a nicely judged bow, the kind you give to female foreigners of relatively low socio-economic status. Japan would treat me with respect but would never let me forget that I was *gaijin*, unalterably different.*

I wasn't sure what frightened me more: being different for a year, or finding out that I didn't feel different at all.

Either way, I thought, as I fell back into jet-lagged sleep, I'm going to be shaken, and by more than a minor earthquake.

---

* *Gaijin*, pronounced "*guy*-jean," means foreigner; literally, "outsider person." It's an abbreviation; the full word is *gaikokujin*.

Two

A COMPANY OF DRAGONS

The next few days passed in a blur of impressions. Traffic, clouds, crowds, rain. Smells of cherry blossom, boiling noodles, tatami mats, stinky drains. The clackety-clack of passing trains; the tapping of women's high heels on pavement. In the department stores, raspberry-pink microwave ovens and lime-green refrigerators. Tens of thousands of people on the streets. I'm mildly phobic about even lightly populated public spaces, so the thousands of people were a problem. I was learning to calm myself by reciting silently a short poem by Ezra Pound—"The apparition of these faces in the crowd: Petals on a wet, black bough." Petals were good. Petals weren't threatening.

What else? Billboards and shop signs I couldn't read. Narrow maze-like streets lined with countless cubby-hole shops. Seafood. Lots of seafood.

A few days after the earthquake, my new colleagues gave a party for me at the Saffron restaurant in Kichijoji, a shopping district near our office in Takaido. The Saffron was in a base-

17

ment. Most restaurants in Tokyo are in basements, I was to learn. There isn't room enough to put them all at street level.

Accompanied by Paul and Tessa, I walked into a warm dark room full of statues with big breasts, lanterns in amber glass, a glazed giant sea-turtle, and a selection of huge oil paintings depicting nude white women in an era when cellulite was considered sexy. "It's a Continental restaurant," Paul explained, guiding me to our table. Yes, but which continent? Over the table hung a fishnet full of shells. Atop the table, displayed on platters, were the shells' former occupants, all glazed eyes and neatly curled tentacles.

Three days in Japan and already my Sophisticated World Traveler image was slipping. I'd believed I had eclectic tastes in food because I liked foreign food in California. But the food at the Saffron restaurant bore scant resemblance to the Japanese food at "Benihana of Tokyo" in Cupertino, California. Benihana may come from Tokyo, but judging from the amount of beef he serves, he arrived in California after an extended stay in the Midwest.

I looked at the ill-favored life-forms on the table in front of me. My mind told my stomach, "This is tasty food, this is nutritious food." My stomach replied, "Shut up and get me a pizza." I don't like admitting that my stomach has more clout than my mind, but I ate so little at my "welcome to Japan" party that Miyuki Suzuki, our group's secretary, apologized for not having ordered more suitable food. In a pattern that would soon became familiar to me, a Japanese person was assuming the burden of my deficiencies.

I assured her that it didn't matter, there was plenty of food I could eat and I wasn't hungry anyway. I tried to be convincing because I liked Miyuki. She made me feel tall; I'm only five feet four, but she came just up to my shoulder. Never mind that she also made me feel old (she was twenty-four) and plain, with her flawless skin, perfect features, and wavy long black hair.

She was soft-spoken, courteous, and intelligent. She had gradu-
ated from Keio, the top private university in Japan, and her
English was excellent.

It seemed obvious to us Americans that Miyuki was wasted
as a secretary, but in Japan in 1985, even the brightest and best-
educated women took jobs as "office ladies." Miyuki didn't
seem to mind serving tea to her colleagues every morning and
afternoon, any more than she had minded translating my dinner
speech into Japanese.

I'd rehearsed the speech, but there hadn't been time to
memorize it. I had to read it. "*Pāti-ni-kite kurete arigatō
gozaimasu.* (Thank you for attending this party.)" I couldn't
tell whether my new colleagues understood, but they applauded
politely. I bowed, sat down, and filled another bowl with rice.

"Good *speech*," said the young man next to me.

"Thank you."

"Nakamura," said the young man, blinking behind his black-
rimmed glasses.

"I'm sorry?"

"My *name* is Nakamura."

He was in his mid-twenties, a small man even for a Japanese, with something nervous and alive in his face. I told him,
"My name is Rhiannon-*san*."

Nakamura turned pink and looked away, apparently to study
an oil painting in which a scantily draped woman was strenu-
ously resisting the advances of a faun. There was something
different about him, something that set him apart from the two
dozen men around the table who all looked alike to me with
their golden skin, black hair, dark eyes.

He turned back to me and I spotted the difference. He was
the first Japanese man I'd seen who had a mustache.

"You can call me '*Yoz*,'" he said.

"Really? Paul said I should call my male colleagues by their
last names."

He nodded vigorously. "For *most* people I *think* that is true, but I am so *different*, you see! So I *prefer* to be called by my nickname."*

"Well, okay, Yoz."

"How do you like *Japan* so far?"

"It's interesting. I'm learning a lot about myself." A nice self-centered answer.

"Maybe you *didn't* enjoy the earthquake last night." Yoz spoke English fluently, but with frequent and oddly-placed stresses. Listening to him was like taking a child armed with a pin into a room full of balloons. You never knew when a word was going to pop.

"Do you have a lot of earthquakes?" I asked. I tried to sound blasé about it. After all, I'd spent most of my life on top of the San Andreas fault.

"*Yes!*" replied my new colleague, with enthusiasm. "One almost every *day*. In the old *legends* we have *written* that the islands of *Japan* are riding on the *back* of a catfish. When this so-called catfish moves his tail—*boom!*"

"A catfish," I repeated.

He frowned. "Some legends say, *not* a catfish, but . . . Miyuki-*san!*" He fired off a question that Miyuki answered in a soft voice. He turned back to me. "*Dragon.*"

I was jet-lagged and very hungry. There were only four women in the SPN group: Miyuki and another secretary, Tessa, and me. All men were strangers. Talk about your dragons! Cigarette fire gleamed in their hands. Smoke poured out of their mouths. Their speech was an incomprehensible, low-volume

---

* A word about Japanese names. We Westerners called most of our colleagues "[surname]-*san*." Some of our female colleagues asked to be called "[first name]-*san*." *San*, an honorific similar to our "Mr." or "Ms.," was never omitted, except with Yoz. In this book, for the sake of greater readability, I've omitted the honorific except in conversation.

roar. I would never learn their names. I would never be able to tell them apart. I would not make any friends. I felt as hollow as the shells above my head.

I stood up and began to work my way around the table. I asked each man his name, repeated it, bowed, and shook his hand. They'd had enough to drink that it made them laugh, watching the face of each fellow as I reached for his hand, and I realized that I was embarrassing them because the Japanese don't shake hands, don't touch each other much and certainly don't touch strange foreign women, but it was too late, I was halfway around the table. It would be worse now to stop than to keep going.

So I kept going, under the shells, past the big-breasted statues and the oil paintings and the amber lanterns, through the smoke and the embarrassment and the shouts of laughter, and I could tell that although I was mispronouncing their names and making them shake my hand, my new colleagues weren't upset with me. My behavior wasn't proper, but they could see beyond the behavior to the impulse that had prompted it. They agreed, it seemed, with E.M. Forster, "Only connect."

I sat down again. I felt flushed and dizzy, as if I had walked a lot farther than around a restaurant table.

Three

"BURST, YOU LITTLE BLOSSOMS!"

I spent my first month in Japan at the Century Hyatt Hotel. Every morning I put on my *yukata*, the blue-and-white cotton robe provided by the hotel, and called Room Service for cornflakes, raisin toast, and coffee with hot milk. While I ate, I looked out my picture window at Tokyo stretching gray and featureless all the way to the horizon. There certainly seemed to be a lot of Tokyo. Then I showered, dressed, and rode the glass elevator down to the lobby, where I walked past the bell-boys wishing me "Good morning, sir!" and out the front door to the taxi stand.

Tokyo taxi drivers keep their cars immaculate—they get out and buff them up between fares—and they wear white gloves and are very civil, but don't let that fool you. They're maniacs. As I sat stiffly in the back seat, regretting the absence of seatbelts and wondering which gods I should be praying to, Shinto or Buddhist, my taxi drivers signaled left and turned right, changed lanes without signaling at all, and told me they knew where the Inokashira Dōri was when they didn't have the least idea and had to stop to ask someone for directions.

The Hewlett-Packard Japan office in Takaido was on the Inokashira Dōri, a street that is noteworthy because it has a name. Most streets in Tokyo are nameless. Addresses usually consist of the *ku* (ward); the *chome* (district); the *ban* (lot number); and the *go* (building number, or in some cases, the age of the building). Unless your destination is famous, there are only two ways for your driver to learn where it is: you can give him a detailed map, or you can name a nearby landmark and then direct him the rest of the way. Miyuki drew a map for me and it worked pretty well, except when I got a driver who didn't know where the Inokashira Dōri was. I couldn't tell him, so he'd have to drive around until he found someone who looked as if he'd know. This was usually a policeman. Fortunately, Tokyo is well stocked with policemen.

You have never seen anyone more relieved than a Tokyo taxi driver who has finally managed to deliver a foreign passenger to the correct destination. (My ancestors be praised! I will not be saddled with this *gaijin* for all eternity! I will not have to take her home and let her stay with my family!) Some of my drivers were so overjoyed that they actually accepted tips, although most of them refused. (I don't want your money! Just let me back on the street, where I will pass the next five hundred foreigners who try to stop me!)

One day toward the end of April, when I'd been in Japan for about ten days, I said "Sayōnara" to another relieved taxi driver and plodded upstairs to the SPN room on the second floor. This was a cheerless rectangle with a low ceiling, furnished with gray carpeting, tan metal desks, and shoulder-high partitions covered in beige industrial-strength fabric. As such, it wasn't that much different from a software office in Silicon Valley, except that there weren't any plants, posters, calendars with pretty pictures, Bloom County and Far Side cartoons, photos of kids or sweethearts. No personal touches at all, except for the stuffed animals that rested on a couple of the terminals.

At least I assume they were resting. I never saw them do a lick of work.

Also different from home: no blue jeans, running shoes, or T-shirts. The men wore suits, taking off their jackets (but never their ties) when they got to work. The women wore skirts and dresses, never trousers. And no snacks sitting around, no jars of candy or bags of chips or cookies. Eating at your desk was against company policy. I did it anyway. None of my Japanese colleagues did.

The room smelled like green tea and cigarette smoke and it was always full of people, the "dragons" from the Saffron restaurant. Most of them were young men in their twenties and early thirties, whom I thought of as "the lads." For my Japanese colleagues in general—lads, secretaries, and managers—I came up with another term, "the Tomodachi."* It made them sound a bit like a *yakuza* gang, but that couldn't be helped.

It had taken me only a few days to learn their names. Their last names, that is. I never used their first names, and certainly not nicknames. You'll have grasped that, in a culture in which you are asked to address a twenty-two-year-old colleague as "Mr. Nagura," you don't suddenly start calling him "Nags." But I did invent monikers for several of the lads, and for this I blame my family. We're the kind of people who attach names to cars and other inanimate objects. My first personal computer, the one I had in Japan, was called "Bunter." My father's Volkswagen beetle was "Methuselah." My grandmother's car was "Oleander." No doubt my distant ancestors were in the habit of naming their plows, their coal-mining lamps, and, moving farther back in time, their primitive stone tools. ("This be Moog. Moog sharp. Me use Moog hit things.")

The lads' nicknames were "for my eyes only," never spoken or even revealed. They were based on inferences and su-

---

* *Tomodachi*, pronouced toe-moe-*dah*-chee, means "friend" in Japanese.

perficialities because that's all I had to go on. If I'd learned sufficient Japanese, I might have discovered eventually that I'd misjudged them. Funakura, for example, had about him the sort of rock-solid reliability that I associate with the name "George," as in the Father of Our Country. You could picture him owning up instantly to having chopped down the cherry tree, except that he would never have touched the tree in the first place. Trustworthy, honorable, dependable, kind . . . it's possible that "George" Funakura had a secret life riddled with vice, but I doubt it.

As I walked into the SPN office, George was talking to "Stars" Kikuchi, a bushy-haired lad who spent his holidays in far-flung places, viewing comets and other astronomical phenomena. Stars was a sweet-natured, generous young man, eager to share his hobby with others. He once offered to show me a phenomenon, in company with several of the lads, but since it involved getting up well before the crack of dawn—actually at around the crack of midnight—I declined.

Spats and the Imp had their heads bent over some printout. Spats (Kiyosawa) was dapper, slim, dark-skinned. He talked fast and he moved fast, with a kind of built-in grace, like a Japanese Fred Astaire. A cigarette burned in his slender fingers. The Imp was Kurokawa, our prankster, who told jokes, mugged, and laughed a lot, a loud cackle. He had arched eyebrows, round specs, thick hair that tended to part itself down the middle, and a big, face-splitting smile.

"Teddy" Iwamoto, who was writing the Japanese documentation for the SPN software, was my idea of the boy next door, friendly, open, enthusiastic about getting to know us Westerners. He was on his way now to the computer room, accompanied by Iizuka, our good-looking systems guru. Mr. Goodwrench, I called him, because he was always fixing software problems for Tessa and me.

"Fingers" Katayama was turning out code at blinding speed. A small, wiry fellow with a tendency to giggle, Fingers was the only person in the office who typed faster than I did. He was one of the lads who kept a stuffed animal on his terminal. Bilingual Bobby Borromeo, who was part American and a devoted family man, nodded and said, "Hi." Miyuki looked up from her work and said, "Good morning, Rhiannon-*san*."

As I headed into the cubicle that I shared with Tessa, in the right-hand corner against the back wall, Yoz lit one cigarette with the remains of another and followed me in. "*Good* morning! How *are* you today?"

"*Genki desu, o-kage sama de. Yoz-san wa?* (I'm fine, thanks. How are you?)"

"*Genki desu.*"

"Where's Tessa?"

"Now she and *Paul* are meeting with *Ito-san.*"

Ito-*san* was the head honcho, the big cheese, the number-one Tomodachi . . . or to put it another way, the overall manager of the SPN group. A man of fifty, he was very reserved, very correct. If he'd been English, he'd have been one of those old-fashioned types in a bowler hat and an old school tie. He reminded me of the character in *Carry On, Jeeves* who had "such a knack of making a fellow feel like a waste-product." Ito-*san* didn't make me feel like a waste-product, exactly, but there was something about the way he looked at me that had me checking myself in the ladies' room immediately afterward for cornflakes in my teeth or a bra-strap showing. He didn't speak much English and I got the impression, perhaps mistaken, that he wasn't thrilled about having to work with foreigners. I never gave Ito-*san* a nickname, and when I try to write his name without the *san*, I feel him looking at me again, and I go back and add the missing three letters.

I wondered what Paul and Tessa were saying to Ito-*san*. Not much, probably. They had been studying Japanese for a year, but they were far from fluent. I was sure I'd be speaking rings around them in no time.

"Ikeda-*san* has *called* a marketing meeting this morning," Yoz added. That would be Kenichi Ikeda, our group's marketing manager—a job he shared with Paul.

"*Ah sō desu ka.*"* I looked guiltily at my watch. HPJ had flex time, unusual in Japan, but we were supposed to be at work by 9:45. It was 10:15. "What time is the meeting?"

"*Jū-ichi-ji.*"

"Um . . . eleven?" I'd had three days of Berlitz lessons in San Francisco before moving to Japan. They were coming in handy.

"*Hai, sō desu.* (Yes, that's right.)"

"Okay, Yoz, thanks."

"*Dō itashimashite.* (You're welcome.)"

Yoz went back to his cubicle. I stuffed my handbag in the bottom drawer of my desk and walked two steps to the windows. We had the usual Tokyo view: a high-rise apartment building—gray concrete disfigured with long stains—and a few scrawny, discouraged-looking trees. The view didn't bother Tessa but it did bother me.

"Excuse me, Rhiannon-*san*." It was Ikeda speaking. He was my boss, along with Paul, but he was apologetic about disturbing my contemplation of the scene outside the window. I skimmed hastily over to my chair and sat down.

"*Ohayō gozaimasu,* Ikeda-*san* (Good morning)," I said, switching on my terminal under cover of my greeting.

Ikeda smiled. It was not the sort of smile that says, *You don't fool me a bit, Miss Tardy-boots.* It was the sort of smile that says, *It's okay, take your time.* An affable man with a broad, handsome face, Ikeda had worked in California and seemed to like Americans, even ones who didn't get to work on time. Although he was my age, thirty-seven, and looked even younger,

---

* An all-purpose phrase that serves the same purpose as our "Really?" or "Oh yeah?" A shorter phrase, *Ah sō desu,* means "Okay" or "Right."

I related to him as to an older person. He was a manager, after all, and the father of a six-year-old daughter.

"So . . . Rhiannon *san*, the marketing group is having a meeting at eleven o'clock."

"Yes, Yoz told me."

"Ah, good! Then you can be able to attend?"

Dear Ikeda-*san*, your company has just paid me two thousand dollars to move to Tokyo and is about to set me up in an apartment, furnish it, pay the rent, and give me a tax-free Cost of Living Allowance in addition to my salary, and so far all I've done for you is appear at the office, usually late, and stare gloomily out the window. Yes, I think I may be able to attend your meeting.

"Of course, Ikeda-*san*!" I said brightly.

"Thank you very much."

He left. I revolved slowly in my chair to face the windows. Ugly, ugly apartment building. Cigarette smoke drifted over the partition: Yoz had just lit up another one. A high-pitched voice cut across the subdued murmurs—that would be Fingers—and then I heard the Imp's crow-cackle laugh. I revolved back On my computer screen, the cursor blinked silently, white on a black background. Blink! Another precious, irreplaceable second of my life had passed. Blink! Another second. Blink! Blink! Blink!

I typed, "I'M BORED!" and pressed the Enter key.

UNKNOWN COMMAND NAME (CIERR 975), the computer responded.

What had Paul been thinking when he wrote, "We need you desperately?"

My job was to document, in English, a set of Japanese enhancements to American software, HP's Semiconductor Productivity Network (SPN). I found this confusing at first. The enhancements had been requested by a Japanese company, one of HPJ's customers. To my simple mind it seemed to follow, as the night the day, that what would be required was documentation in Japanese. (The stuff that Teddy was writing.)

I had said so to Paul during my preview trip in December. He had replied that, as I would know if I hadn't spent the past six months jaunting about Europe instead of attending to my duties in California, the enhancements were destined to become part of the standard product. Every SPN user would have them—Americans, Europeans, Koreans—a veritable United Nations of users, most of whom couldn't read Japanese. Because, let's face it, no one but the Japanese *can* read Japanese, whereas, happily for us, lots of people can read English. Especially if their jobs depend on it.

"The entire user community will be relying on your documentation," Paul had said, "to understand Shop Floor Control and the new station/operation relationship." If he hoped to intimidate me with language like that, he had sadly misjudged his writer. My ambition in younger years was to write the *Uncle Tom's Cabin* of my time, a book that would put an end to racism, poverty, misogyny, and war while also bringing in substantial royalties. I pictured myself accepting the Pulitzer and the Nobel Prize for Peace on the same day; a practical daydream, because I'd only have to buy one outfit. Okay, I hadn't achieved my ambition yet, but I was not likely to be fazed by the thought of some Belgian semiconductor engineer poring over my account of Stream 6 data collection.

I got to my feet and walked down the row of back-wall cubicles to Duncan Marshall's. Duncan, a gifted systems analyst, was in charge of designing and programming the enhancements. He had told me, a few days after I got to Tokyo, that the new code "wasn't firm enough for documentation."* This was bad news for me, because Paul didn't seem to have anything else for me to do.

---

* Duncan had to coordinate the work his team produced with the SPN office at home, which led to a series of wretched complications and delays, not the fault of the SPN group in Japan.

I stuck my head into his cubicle. "Hi, Duncan. Any joy?"

"I'm afraid not," Duncan said.

"Software is supposed to be soft," I suggested.

Duncan grinned. With his rough beard and blazing blue eyes, he looked like a dangerously intelligent pirate. "Not *this* soft," he said. "Have you read the specs I gave you?"

"The character development is weak, but the plot's terrific."

"Glad you approve." He went back to his printout. Duncan was not a man who could be tempted into idle chatter on company time.

So much the worse for me. There were only five Foreign Service Employees in the SPN group: Duncan, Paul, Tessa, Dan Uno, and myself. Dan was Japanese-American and should have looked at home in Japan, but he didn't. He walked like an American, swinging his arms, taking up space, and he sat like an American, sprawling over his chair instead of perching neatly on it. I'm a sprawler myself, and I could have chatted with Dan indefinitely, but his cubicle was next to Duncan's and Duncan was his boss.

I returned to my cubicle and found Tessa typing at her terminal, looking, as usual, like a passion-flower trying to pass itself off as a daisy. Tessa was only twenty-nine, but she had played even more roles than I had. She had been a secretary and a belly-dancer (it was easier to picture her in the latter role). She was now playing technical writer. This was a challenge given her odd-ball approach to the English language. Since meeting Tessa I had started a collection of her malapropisms. "Hey, look at that cow chewing its cod," was one of my favorites. Also, "You should've seen her, Nano, she was dressed to the kilt!" Tessa wrote the way she spoke, which made her documents exciting to edit, but she could find her way around an HP3000 mini-computer like nobody's business, whereas I could barely remember how to turn my terminal on. She had blue-green eyes, long mahogany-colored hair, and a body that had several ways of calling attention to itself even when she was just sitting there typing.

We were friends, but there was tension between us. For complicated reasons, I tried in those days to live mainly in my head, as if nothing below the neck mattered except on rare special occasions. The image that I wanted to project was cool and classy—Sophisticated World Traveler. And there sat Tessa in the same cubicle with me, warm and earthy and juicy, shocking me with every other sentence. She was casual, spontaneous, extroverted. I was deliberate, controlled, and introspective to a fault.

"I'm not a party animal," I had told her once, defensively.

"Nano," she had replied—it was Tessa who had given me the nickname "Nano"—"you're not even a party *vegetable*."

Today she acknowledged my entrance with a blithe, "How's it goin', Nano?"

"No work yet."

"Bummer."

"There's a marketing meeting at eleven."

"Mmm-hmm." She was typing furiously.

By five o'clock that afternoon, I had attended the marketing meeting, sent six e-mail messages to colleagues in California, and written a couple of haiku that I was rather proud of.

> I dreamed last night
> I found a tentacle in my cornflakes
> Culture shock

> The clock's hands move
> As if Godzilla himself
> Were trying to stop them

Dusk was falling outside. Tessa was still typing. I sat at my desk flipping through a book of Japanese proverbs.*

---

* I have learned recently that this book, written by a foreigner, contains several mistakes

"*Aki no ōgi*," I said.

"Hmm?"

"It's a Japanese proverb. It means, 'a fan in autumn.'"*

"Mmm."

"It's what the Japanese say about a useless thing."

Tessa looked up. "You're not useless, Nano."

"Want to see my haiku?"

"I thought you were reading the specs again."

"I did. I still don't understand them."

"You will."

I flipped a few pages in the book of proverbs. "*Kago no tori, kumo wo shitau.* Caged birds yearn for clouds."

Tessa sighed, typed a couple of commands, and switched off her terminal. "Let's go."

"Go where?"

"I'm taking you home for dinner."

She scribbled a note for Paul, who was meeting with Ikeda, and we walked out into the misty late-April dusk. "We'll take the train," she said.

"Taxi."

"Nano, once you've moved into your apartment, the company won't pay for taxis anymore and you'll have to use trains, so you might as well start now. Anyway, it's more fun, you know? More real."

"Taxis are fun. Taxis are real."

"Taxis are expensive."

We walked fifteen minutes to Takaido station, mounted several flights of stairs, and jammed into a standing-room-only train. It was real all right, but it wasn't fun. "We'll get off at Inokashira Koen and walk through the park," Tessa said. "Just wait till you see the cherry trees, Nano. You're so lucky to be here for *sakura*!"**

---

* *Aki no ōgi* is actually *karo tōsen* ("a stove in summer, a fan in winter").

** Cherry blossom time.

It was dark and cold. We were two women alone in a park at night. To my way of thinking, these did not represent ideal conditions for viewing cherry blossoms. "We're perfectly safe," Tessa said. I didn't believe her. Perfect safety is not a concept I can relate to.

We trudged along. Rain started falling, splotching the brown leather boots I had bought in London. "My boots are getting wet," I fussed. "My best boots, Tessa. They're going to be ruined!"

Tessa tugged my arm and pointed up into the cherry trees.

Big as houses, they spread their branches over our heads. The park lamps shone through them, lighting up clouds of pink and leafy green against the black sky. Wind shook the trees and petals fell like rain, rain fell like petals, the air was full of flowers and water. I flung out my arms and started spinning around under the trees. "A dance for *sakura*!"

"An ode to *sakura*!" Tessa cried. She thought for a minute and then chanted:

Burst, you little blossoms!
Let yourselves be seen!
Come out on your black branches.
Explosions, explosions of dreams!

If there was anyone else in the park that night—a housewife hurrying home from the shops in Kichijoji, a group of salary-men on their way to a bar for after-work drinks—what did they think of the two white women twirling around under the giant cherry trees in the rain? Did they shrug and tell themselves that all *gaijin* are crazy? Did they think that we were drunk? Or did they recognize that what intoxicated us was a mood, fragile as a blossom, born of friendship and beauty and strangeness?

Next morning, I handed my boots to the shoeshine man at the Century Hyatt Hotel. *"Sakura desu,"* I said sadly, pointing to the pink fragments pasted onto the dirty, water-stained leather.

"Ah sō desu," he replied.

When I picked up the boots that evening, they were so shiny I could see my face in them.

Four

☉

THE HOUSE OF CLEAR WATER

Miyuki had taken me apartment-hunting during my preview trip in December, 1984. She had walked miles through the rain beside me in her high-heeled shoes, holding her umbrella— characteristically, I had forgotten to pack one—over my head rather than hers. We looked at several apartments in Kichijoji, small, depressing places with telephone poles so close to the living room windows that you could reach out and touch the transformers.

"I am sorry, Rhiannon-*san*," Miyuki said. "These are not suitable."

Next day we went in the opposite direction from the office, east instead of west on the Inokashira Line, and got off two stops down at Nishi Eifuku.

We walked down a narrow street packed with shops, crossed the Inokashira Dōri, walked west one block, and turned up another street. This one was so narrow that the English would call it a lane. It was still raining. Water dripped on us from the bare limbs of huge cherry trees. They would be covered with blossom, Miyuki told me, when I moved to Japan in April.

After three short blocks, Miyuki said, "There is the building, Rhiannon-*san*. *Esta Shimizu*. Shimizu is the name of the owner."

"What does '*shimizu*' mean?" I asked, brushing raindrops off the sleeve of my wool jacket.

"It means something like 'clear water.'"

By Western standards, Esta Shimizu was not attractive. Flat-roofed, decked out with small elliptical balconies and covered with square white tiles, it looked like a giant's bathroom turned inside out. It was only three stories tall but it loomed whitely over the traditional tile-roofed houses in the lane.

We greeted Mr. Shimizu—that is, Miyuki did; I was limited to bows and smiles—and he led us up an outside staircase to the top floor. The apartment's front door was made of thick gray metal, which suggested a certain amount of paranoia on the part of the builder. Or was there something Miyuki wasn't telling me about the Nishi Eifuku neighborhood?

Mr. Shimizu opened the metal door for me and I walked in. The apartment was brand-new. Polished hardwood floors shone like fresh butterscotch. The walls were covered in off-white vinyl paper, a precaution against summer humidity. Two sliding glass doors in the living room led onto slender balconies. The views ranged from uninspired to ugly, but there weren't any transformers nearby.

Best of all, the House of Clear Water was within walking distance of the office. I knew already that I wanted to spend as little time as possible on Tokyo trains.

I nodded and smiled and bowed. Mr. Shimizu took Miyuki and me to his apartment on the ground floor and gave us cups of hot green tea. Rain was falling harder than ever when Miyuki and I walked back to Nishi Eifuku station, but I hardly noticed. I was mentally arranging furniture in my new apartment.

After I moved to Japan, during that first month at the Century Hyatt Hotel, I spent hours studying furniture catalogues and drawing floor plans. I was so determined to get everything right that when Miyuki said I could have a refrigerator in white, avocado, or maroon, I was unable to function for several hours, although you'd think the choice would have been obvious.

I got the fridge and a bed first. On the day they were delivered, a Sunday, I moved into my new apartment. The stuff I'd had shipped from California came later that afternoon. I leaned over the living-room balcony and shot photographs of my beloved computer, Bunter, as it appeared from the back of the truck.

With something to sleep on, something to keep food in, and something to write with, my basic needs were met. While I waited for the rest of my new furniture to be delivered, I sat on the floor—very Japanese—and hung my clothes from the metal frames over the sliding glass doors. It was depressing to see so much of my wardrobe, but at least the clothes weren't getting wrinkled.

My apartment was a 3-LDK* and contained about 570 square feet. In those days, the city government's minimum standard for a family of four was 540 square feet, or 135 square feet per person. By Japanese standards I was living in a mansion.

I used the LDK as a kitchen. It came with a sink, a grill, and two burners. The Japanese don't use ovens much but I requested one from Miyuki and it was duly purchased and delivered.

The largest of the three remaining rooms was my living and dining room. The smallest was my guest room and study. The third room, where I slept, had a peaked cedar ceiling and a six-tatami-mat floor.** The mats were trimmed in green and

---

* LDK stands for living room/dining room/kitchen. In Tokyo houses and apartments, one room often serves all three functions. A 3-LDK apartment has three rooms in addition to the LDK.
** Tatami mats, about three feet by six feet, are the usual unit of measurement for Japanese rooms. They are made of tightly woven rice straw covered with woven rush grass and bound with cotton cloth.

gold ribbon, the walls were moss-green, and there was a long closet on one wall with sliding paper doors painted in a green-and-gold design.

The bathroom had inner and outer rooms. The outer room contained a sink, a medicine cabinet, a washing machine and dryer. A folding door led to an inner room, completely water-proof, that housed a deep Japanese-style tub and a shower head that could be attached to the wall at several levels. It wasn't beautiful; there was no window, no view; but functionally it was the finest bathroom I've ever used. It had such a powerful extractor fan that I could hang wet clothes on a rack over the bathtub and find them dry four hours later.

For their apartment, Paul and Tessa had picked out drapes in ten minutes and taken furniture from the HPJ warehouse, remnants of a departed Foreign Service Employee. But I had spent years in cheap American apartments (avocado kitchens, orange acrylic shag carpeting) and English flats (red and gold wallpaper, turquoise paisley carpeting, maroon upholstery—all in the same room). Since HPJ would pay for most of the furni-ture, here was a chance to live among nice things of my own choosing at someone else's expense. I couldn't believe my luck.

My own choosing, I discovered, ran to simple pine furni-ture; lots of mirrors, candles, plants, and baskets; and natural fabrics. Miyuki was my aide-de-camp. I hope that she found helping me furnish an apartment a welcome change from her other duties, because I certainly took up a lot of her time. She gave me catalogues, placed orders, and arranged for delivery. She also introduced me to Tokyu *depāto*—department store— in Kichijoji, an act roughly equivalent to that of taking a pil-grim to Mecca. "The main store is in Shibuya," she told me. Shibuya was the last stop east on the Inokashira Line and thus easy to get to. An entire floor of the Shibuya store was devoted to traditional Japanese crafts (pottery, glassware, kimonos, lacquerware), and both the Kichijoji and Shibuya stores featured changing exhibits of paintings, sculpture, and antiques. I wasn't shopping, I rationalized, I was engaging in cross-cultural research.

The sliding glass doors in my living room had double curtain rods. With Miyuki's help, I had two sets of curtains made at a shop called Fabrications. The main curtains were hunter-green cotton, with a pattern of tiny cream-colored leaves. For the inner, next-to-the-glass curtains, I had to shop harder. Finally, I found a sheer off-white cotton fabric figured with paler, almost transparent leaves.

On weekends I shopped for rugs, lamps, cushions, and mirrors. I loved shopping in Japan. The clerks and owners called out "*Irasshaimase!* (Welcome!)" when I entered their stores. They wrapped every purchase, beautifully, in paper folded on the diagonal. If the item was large or heavy, they tied string around it and made a handle out of the string. If the item was really large or heavy, they delivered it. Free. Any day of the week. When they gave me my purchases, they bowed.

When I needed a break from decorating, I could walk a few short blocks to the grounds of my neighborhood shrine. Six thousand azalea bushes lined the stone-paved approach to the Divine Gate. The Omiya Hachiman Shrine was auspicious for matchmaking, easy childbirth and the bringing-up of children, none of which I intended to experience in Japan. Comforting, though, to learn that it was also the shrine of traffic safety. Perhaps I'd be safe from taxi drivers after all.

Dan Uno, the Japanese-American in our group, helped me buy a stereo in Akihabara, Tokyo's center for electronics shopping. Dan's Japanese wasn't exactly fluent, but he spoke enough to say "Big speakers" and "What do you think she's made of, money?" In an electronics shop, I handed over eleven hundred dollars from my "relocation allowance,"* in cash. In those days,

---

* A Foreign Service Employee perk, intended to cover the cost of moving. We got them both coming and going.

most Japanese used cash or bank transfers instead of checks or credit cards.

The components were delivered a few days later. I tried to persuade the delivery men to set up the stereo for me, and I still think I could have, if only I'd been able to say anything they could comprehend. As it was, they ignored my enticing gestures, set down the boxes, handed me a pile of instruction booklets, and left. Technical writers are notorious for their reluctance to read documentation,* and the instruction booklets weren't much help anyway, being written in Japanese. Using a table knife as a screwdriver and all the determination in my nature, I got the job done. An hour later, Bruce Springsteen's voice was ringing through the House of Clear Water, informing the unfortunate residents, as if they needed to be told, that I was "born in the U.S.A."

The next afternoon, I went to a nearby electric-goods store to buy a vacuum cleaner. I pointed to the model of my choice. The shopkeepers, a husband and wife, offered it to me in pale blue or burgundy, but I insisted on white, like the one on display outside the shop, because I wanted it to match my refrigerator. They tried to explain that they had no vacuum cleaners in white, only the display model, but I didn't understand them. Finally, instead of doing the sensible thing—hitting me over the head with an attachment—they brought in the display model, spent fifteen minutes cleaning it and another fifteen minutes demonstrating its functions, and then gave me a twenty percent discount off the price I'd already agreed to pay. All this with as many bows and smiles as if they actually wanted to see me again, instead of hoping that the first time I used the vacuum cleaner I'd suck myself up the nozzle.

A week later, the rest of my furniture arrived. For more than an hour, two delivery men carried assorted pieces of pine

---

* "RTFM," we've been known to tease fellow writers when they ask technical questions. The initials stand for "Read the fucking manual."

up three flights of stairs and placed it carefully where I indicated. It was a hot day and they were dripping sweat by the time they had finished.

"*Beeru?* (Beer?)" I offered, pointing to the refrigerator. "*Samui desu.* (It's cold.)"

They smiled and shook their heads. "Driving!" they explained.*

I tried to give them a three-thousand yen tip—about twenty dollars.

Again, they shook their heads. "Wear-come to Japan," they said, and took their leave.

All the furniture fit where I'd planned it. Around the wall in my kitchen, I created a frieze of postcards from European museums and galleries. I hung old family photographs in my living room, to be joined in time by a group of Japanese prints. At night, with the hunter-green curtains drawn and a bouquet of flowers on my grandmother's antique trunk, the place looked like a magazine ad. Lamplight glowed on the polished floors and the stripped-pine furniture.

Paul and Tessa thought I went way over the top with my apartment. So did Duncan, no doubt, if he ever considered the matter. Not that I spent too much of HPJ's money, but that I wasted too much time. All those hours drawing floor plans and shopping when I could have been teaching myself COBOL, touring museums, or learning Japanese verbs.

Some people really are portable. They can travel the world alone with just a few things in a rucksack and never feel a qualm of self-doubt, because everything they need to feel like themselves is inside them. Most of us, though, require props. Paul and Tessa didn't need baskets and natural-fiber curtains, but then they had each other. Duncan had his wife, Linette. And all

---

* "If we are caught driving after *drinking*," Yoz told me, "the newspaper will print our *name*, and that will bring shame to our *family* and our *company*. So I *think* we will never do this."

of them were doing the work they wanted to do. None of them, as far as I ever learned, was tormented with ambition to do something else. When they got up in the morning and went to HPJ, it was because they wanted to be there, managing and writing code and documenting software. I wanted to stay home and use Bunter to write a novel.

It was Miyuki who understood. "I like your taste," she said in her soft voice, surveying the finished apartment. Just four words, but somehow she conveyed that we had spent the past six weeks putting together a collection of necessary props. The family photos, the art-gallery postcards, the curtains—I needed them all to play my current role, because there was nothing else around to tell me who I was. the House of Clear Water was a refuge, but it was more than that. It was also a mirror.

Five

✝

"THE NAIL THAT STICKS UP . . ."

Blossoms fell from the cherry trees and formed what Tessa called "*sakura* slick," drifts of dried petals in the streets that turned to gray-pink mush underfoot. At the lake in Inokashira Park, baby ducks paddled after their mothers across the green water. The days grew warmer. It was late spring in Tokyo and I was developing a routine.

Alarm off at eight o'clock. Coffee and cereal. Shower. A half-hour walk down the Inokashira Dōri, arriving at the office at around ten. "*Ohayō gozaimasu*" to the Tomodachi. Lunch (crackers, peanut butter, an apple) at my desk, although employees were supposed to eat in the cafeteria downstairs, where exciting treats such as dried seaweed were on offer. Homeward bound ("*Sayōnara*" to the Tomodachi) at about five-thirty, stopping for basic groceries at the Summit supermarket on the Inokashira Dōri. For exotic imports like Shredded Wheat, I had to venture farther afield, a ninety-minute trip to Kichijoji. I found a nearby dry cleaner that did excellent work; the owner totted up my bills on an abacus. To bed late, due to chronic insomnia. Occasional get-togethers with American or Japanese colleagues. A quiet life. A lonely life.

45

I missed my two great comforts, friends and books. I need to look at things written in English the way some people need to drink or gamble. In Tokyo, this meant traveling to Kichijoji to see magazines, and in the other direction to Shinjuku to see books. I didn't buy much; the prices were too high. The presence all around me of inaccessible texts—the Japanese are assiduous readers of everything from comic books (*manga*) to Shakespeare in translation—created a constant itch of frustration, a kind of subliminal mind-tease. Tessa had given me a beautiful antique print of the Seven Gods of Good Fortune— what she called the Seven Happy Gods—sailing through calm waters in a dragon-prowed boat, and I'd hung it in my living room. Whenever I looked at it I saw the gods laughing at me, mocking my inability to read their language. What else did they have to be happy about? It was an awfully crowded boat.

At least I'd been able to bring some books with me. Friends were harder to come by. At home and in England I had a crowd of them. In Tokyo the crowd was reduced to four: Duncan, the Colemans—Tessa and Paul—and Linette, who worked at the HPJ factory in Hachioji. No problem, I thought, before I moved to Japan. We all got along well. Paul and Duncan were old pals; Paul had been best man at the Marshalls' wedding. The two couples lived next door to each other, so I could visit all of them in one trip to Mitaka. I pictured the five of us getting together frequently for dinner parties, nights out on the town (I would flake out early, but I could always get a cab home), and weekend trips to nearby beauty spots. If there were any nearby beauty spots.

But at some point in the winter of 1985, there was a quarrel, and by the time I moved to Japan in April, the two couples were no longer speaking. In the words of a Japanese proverb, they were *inu to saru no naka*, "on bad terms like dogs and monkeys."

There was no way of hiding the estrangement. Everyone knew about it. Over time, the more assertive of the Tomodachi—

Yoz, Spats, Bobby, and the Imp—asked me, in the hushed voices
of people who are shocked by what they are saying, "Rhian-
non-*san*, why don't Paul-*san* and Duncan-*san* talk to each
other?" I couldn't tell them. Paul and Tessa said they didn't
know why Duncan was angry with them, and I never mentioned
the feud to Duncan. I was afraid of getting dragged in and being forced to take sides. Since my job depended on both of them,
I couldn't afford to have either Paul or Duncan mad at me.

The feud hung like a second low ceiling over the SPN office, depressing everyone. On a bad day, Duncan would come
into our cubicle, ask me a friendly question, and leave, ignoring Tessa completely, and Tessa would take out her anger on
me for the rest of the day. She didn't mean to do it but that
didn't make it any easier to bear. On one spectacularly bad day,
Paul, who was Duncan's boss, gave the younger man his performance review at a nearby conference table. Paul was an exacting manager. He had given me the worst performance review I ever got at Hewlett-Packard, so I could only imagine
what he was saying to Duncan. Tessa and I crouched tensely in
our cubicle and didn't even pretend to work. I fiddled with my
hair and Tessa picked at her nails. We heard Paul's voice, a long
rumble. Then Duncan's voice rose—"Bullshit!"—and his chair
scraped back as he jumped up and left the conference table.

Seconds later Paul erupted into our cubicle. "Get your
things!" he said roughly. "Both of you! We're going."

"Where?" I asked. Tessa shushed me and hustled me out of
the office after Paul. We walked past Ito-*san*, who was sitting
alone at the conference table looking stunned. The Japanese do
not quarrel at work. They may dislike or even detest each other,
but they will never let it show. This has been true for hundreds
of years; it was remarked upon by Christian missionaries in the
sixteenth century, such as Alessandro Valignano, a Jesuit priest,
who commented on the absence of "shouting or brawling such
as can be heard in other countries." Ito-*san* had probably never
witnessed such a display of naked emotion, except on televi-

sion or at the movies (and it was hard to imagine Ito-*san* at the movies). He must have felt like a man who's been told to sit on a ton of dynamite and then been handed a flaming stick.

Paul walked so fast to Takaido station that Tessa and I had to jog to keep up with him. We went into the restaurant at the station and Paul ordered wine. Again, I asked the Colemans what the quarrel was about. Again, they said they didn't know.

I didn't believe them. Duncan could be challenging, but he wasn't petty or unfair. If he was angry with the Colemans, there was a reason. Why wouldn't they tell me what it was? I even found myself wondering if Paul had brought me to Tokyo early to replace Linette Marshall as Tessa's friend. Or maybe I was supposed to be a buffer, the person everyone could talk to, the one who could be relied upon to keep her temper: "sense" to everyone else's "sensibility." This seemed unlikely; Paul was very conscientious about his job; but what else was I doing in Tokyo with no work to do, stuck like a cubicle wall between two warring couples?

Blessed may be the peacemakers, but if you've grown up keeping peace in your family you're not likely to be happy about having to do it on the job. I was angry with all three of my colleagues, but especially with Paul and Tessa.

I have never known what to do with anger. Impossible to express it, impossible not to feel it. Another sort of person, the Sophisticated World Traveler, would have knocked Paul's and Duncan's heads together and said, "I can't be happy here with this feud going on. Resolve it." But I couldn't, which made me feel like a weakling, which made me even angrier.

Travel is supposed to enlarge your world. Ultimately, living in Japan did give me new friends, memorable experiences, an abiding interest in another culture. But most of the time my world in Japan felt smaller, not bigger. This was partly my fault. Tokyo has several English-language newspapers, but in a foolish attempt to save money, I never bought them, and of course I couldn't understand the TV broadcasts. It was like being back at sea with my ex-husband, the Merchant Navy officer: the only things that seem real are the ship and your crew-mates. When nothing from the outside world impinges on you, the outside world might as well not exist at all.

One morning, Paul and Tessa got to work late, looking shocked. "It's terrible, Nano," Tessa said shakily. "Challenger exploded."

"What do you mean? What's 'Challenger'?" I had never heard of the space shuttle or any of the people who had died.

Then too, I was used to having a wide choice of people whom I could confide in, kvetch to, talk things over with. In Japan there was no one with whom I could be completely candid. Paul was my boss. Tessa was my boss's wife. Duncan was the one person in the office who could explain the new software to me in words I could understand. In effect, all three were my superiors, and not to be trusted with some of my pent-up emotions, such as my exasperation over the feud or my fear that I'd never understand the new enhancements.

On weekends, I could either see the Colemans, see the Marshalls, roam around Tokyo by myself, or stay home. Most weekends I stayed home and worked on *Terminal Death*. This was the aptly-named mystery novel that I'd begun during my six-month leave of absence in Europe. Just before coming to Japan, I'd finished it, but decided it wasn't good enough. I was now embarked upon a complete new draft. When my novel was going badly, I got depressed. When it was going well, I yearned to be home working on it instead of wasting time at the office. During creative-writing sessions, I told myself that I should be out experiencing Tokyo, and on the rare occasions when I went out to experience Tokyo, I worried that I was showing insufficient dedication to my writing.

It was a mistake to work on *Terminal Death* while I was living in Japan, but it made sense at the time. I disliked being an employee, even for a company as humane as Hewlett-Packard. Getting up early, wearing a badge, being around people all day, handling office politics, restricting myself to two weeks of freedom a year—none of these came easily to me. The thought of being a "salary-woman" for the rest of my life was terrifying. I didn't realize until nearly the end of my stay in Tokyo that everything would change when I got home; that my life after HPJ would be different *because* of HPJ. In writing a mystery novel, I was making a bid to put office work behind me, to salvage the rest of my life. And it couldn't just be a good novel. It would have to earn enough money so that I could live on the proceeds while I wrote my next book. It would have to be a bestseller.

So I had my agenda. Work full-time for HPJ, master the new software, learn Japanese, try not to antagonize either Paul or Duncan, keep Tessa happy, and write a bestselling novel, all in the space of one year. As Yoz would say, no problem, Nano!

After several weeks in the House of Clear Water, it occurred to me that if I rode a bicycle to work, I could save a few more minutes each day for *Terminal Death*. I wheeled the bike I'd had shipped from California to a nearby bicycle shop and, using Japanese, English, and sign language, managed to communicate several important messages. (1) Please inflate my tires. (2) Please attach a light. (3) Please lower the seat. (4) Please sell me a lock.

When I got up the next morning, it was raining. Never mind! *Adventure desu ne!* (It'll be an adventure, won't it!) Like Tessa, I observed Japanese custom and never wore trousers to the office; before I left California, I'd put together a hasty assortment of skirts and dresses. I pulled a full-length hooded poncho over today's freshly laundered, big-skirted dress. There, now I was ready for anything.

The bike was a boy's model, so in order to climb on I had to hitch my slip up to my thighs. My neighbors kindly averted their eyes while I did this. As I pedaled along the Inokashira Dōri, my skirt kept getting caught in the spokes, so I bunched it up in one hand and held it out to the side, like an Edwardian lady. The rain fell harder, and a strong wind started up. My poncho blew open and flapped around me (Edwardian lady with wings). The poncho got caught in the spokes. As I retrieved my errant clothing and bunched it firmly between my thighs, the bike wobbled alarmingly toward oncoming traffic, which I couldn't see because my glasses had steamed up. I let go of the clothing and raised a shaky hand to rub my glasses. The poncho's hood fell down.

I got to work even later than usual, with a flushed face, dripping hair, wet clothes, and smeared glasses. The Tomodachi refrained from comment, although the Imp rolled his eyes at me. Tessa said I looked as if I'd gone over Yosemite Falls in a barrel.

So I put my bike into storage at Esta Shimizu and bought a girl's bicycle with a bell and a basket. Pedaling around the neighborhood, with tiny insects suiciding themselves against my spectacles, I found a narrow street around the corner from my nameless lane, a street that paralleled the Inokashira Dōri all the way to Takaido. I called it Church Street because about a mile down there was a small square church with a wooden cross beside the door. This became my new route to work. It took me fifteen minutes, door-to-door. I had the shortest commute of anyone at HPJ but I still couldn't manage to get there on time.

Before we Americans arrived, our Japanese colleagues had been accustomed to working, heads down all day, in barn-like rooms that lacked partitions or private offices, sharing phones and even computer terminals, while their managers sat at the back of the room and kept an eye on them. As Tessa said, with typical candor, "When we first got here, you couldn't even pick your nose in private."

By the time I arrived, Paul had fought and won the battles of "One Man, One Terminal" and "Let There Be Partitions." The lads were happy with their terminals and indifferent to the partitions, which they didn't much see the point of.

I had to fight other battles by myself. Paul didn't object to the lighting in our office, bare fluorescent tubes that flickered a scant few feet above our heads. When I pointed out that sitting under unshielded fluorescent lights is bad for the eyes and the complexion, Paul shrugged. Most of his craggily handsome face was shrouded in a beard. The beardless bits were covered by glasses. "Hey, no problem!" was his commonsense attitude to premature aging of the skin.

He was likewise resigned to the dangers of sidestream smoke, which the lads produced in endless, stinking quantities. Yoz, a chain-smoker, was a particular menace. He sat on the other side of my cubicle and I tensed every time I heard him click his lighter.

I've got my addictions too, and one of them is complaining. I'm a chain-complainer. But Tessa got fed up with listening to my rants. She urged me to take action instead, so every morning when I arrived, I switched off the lights over our cubicle and opened our two windows. In wandered tentative puffs of air. It wasn't fresh air, exactly, but at least it hadn't been recently exhaled from the lungs of a smoker.

It didn't occur to me that anyone would take exception to my turning off lights and opening windows, but they did. *Deru kugi wa utareru*, says the famous Japanese proverb: "The nail that sticks up must be hammered down."* I was sticking up. Several of the lads commented that our cubicle was "dark." Actually it was flooded with daylight, but apparently natural light didn't count. Ito-*san* commented as well, to Ikeda, who repeated his comments to Paul, who repeated them to me. Although I suspected that this daisy-chain of comment amounted to an order ("Turn on the lights and shut your damned win-

---

* Japanese schools still conduct monthly "moral inspections" at which teachers check the students' hair (no dye, no streaks, no perms allowed), fingernails (no polish), ears (no piercing), and the length of girls' skirts.

dows"), I feigned ignorance. I didn't want to be rude to my Japanese hosts, but I had no intention of being hammered.

Nor were these my only offenses. I also went around for several weeks calling myself "Rhiannon-*san*." As noted earlier, *san* is the Japanese courtesy title, similar to our Mr. and Ms., but applying to both sexes. (That's why the bellboys at the Century Hyatt Hotel kept calling me "sir.") *San* means something like "honorable person," and implying that you believe yourself to be honorable is considered boasting in Japan, although it doesn't sound like much of a boast to American ears.

Bad Japanese Boast	Bad English Boast	Bad American Boast
"I am an honorable person."	"I have, upon occasion, behaved in ways that are not completely devoid of honour."	"I'm the most honorable person in the whole God-damned universe and if you don't believe me I'll blow your head off."

So you shouldn't call yourself *san*, any more than you should say that your wife is accomplished or your husband successful. In Japan, boasting about your family or your possessions is bad form. This makes it tough not to sound rude in Japan, because, let's face it, American conversations tend to consist of one person boasting while another person makes noises such as, "Awright!"

One might hazard a conjecture, based on twenty-odd years of dating them, that not boasting poses a particular problem for American men. But there's a problem for American women, too. When she turns twelve (there's talk of dropping the age to ten, or even eight), every American girl is taken into a room decorated with pinups of celery-stick models and given a script to memorize for use in conversations with other girls. It goes like this:

"God, I'm so fat!"

"No, you're not."

"I'm enormous!"

"You look great."

"I look like a beached whale!"

"You do not."

And so on. Women sometimes use this script in conversations with men—a mistake, because men don't know the script exists, so instead of saying, "No, you're not," they say things like, "Then why did you eat that banana split?"

But Japanese women don't know the script either. If you say "God, I'm so fat!" to a Japanese woman, first of all she will wonder why you're addressing her as God. Then she'll consider how to handle the rest of your sentence. She will reflect that you are, by comparison with her, indeed fat; that Westerners are said to prize honesty and directness; and that if you thought fat was a bad thing you wouldn't eat so much pepperoni pizza. After pondering these points in an effort to construct the most courteous possible reply, she will say, "Ah, yes, Rhiannon-*san*, I have noticed this."

After I'd been in Japan for several months, I realized that I never saw Japanese people blowing their noses. This struck me as odd, because the air pollution in Tokyo kept me honking like an hyperactive fog horn. Did the Japanese have superior sinuses? When I asked Yoz, he didn't understand the phrase "blow your nose," so I whipped out a tissue and gave him a demonstration. "Is that rude?" I demanded.

Yoz turned pink, looked away, and said, "*Iie* (No)." Reassured, I continued to blow my nose on the street, in the office, in Tokyu *depāto*, in coffee shops and restaurants.

Months later, I read in a guidebook that blowing your nose in Japan is unpardonable, scandalous, worse than pissing in public. Even ruder, though, was forcing Yoz to tell me that I'd been rude. Confronted with a choice between hurting my feelings or lying to me, he had chosen to lie like a true Japanese gentleman.

Miyuki was more forthcoming. It was she who told me, gently, that I shouldn't refer to myself as "Rhiannon-*san*." No wonder I'd made Yoz blush at the Saffron restaurant! It was also Miyuki who tipped me off that the flowers I'd been taking as dinner-party gifts—white chrysanthemums—are appropriate only for hospital visits and funerals.

I learned other rules from books. Lots of them had to do with chopstick etiquette. You should never pass food to another person with your chopsticks; this behavior mimics an old ceremony in which the bones of the dead are passed around by family members. (Why are the bones passed around? The book didn't say, and it's the kind of question that keeps you up at night wondering.) You should also refrain from sticking your chopsticks vertically into your rice, because a bowl of rice with chopsticks in this position is offered to the dead in family shrines.

The Japanese say that there are three excuses for bad behavior: being drunk, being a child, and being foreign. I considered this insulting at first, but I came to see it as recognition that unless you've been brought up in the culture, you can't hope to know the rules. Fortunately, as I learned that night at the Saffron, the Japanese are willing to judge you by your intentions, not your conduct. It can wear you down a bit, knowing that people are always having to make allowances for you, but it's better than being written off as a barbarian.

I liked most of the Japanese customs I encountered. Taking my shoes off as soon as I got home made sense; it kept the hardwood floors shining. Never pouring beer or wine for myself at a party, but always waiting for someone else to do it, corrected my American tendency to guzzle. Bowing to people made me feel gracious, and being bowed to was an honor.

I stopped calling myself *san*. I scuttled to the restroom whenever I needed to blow my nose. I didn't miss the "God, I'm so fat" conversations because I didn't feel fat. Without a car, I was obliged to walk or bicycle everywhere, and it's hard to gain weight on white rice.

I'd like to report that I went all the way and gave up boasting as well, but if I did—I'd be boasting. But it didn't matter that I kept forgetting to be humble. There was an excuse for my bad behavior. Perhaps there was even an excuse for the Colemans' and Duncan's. We weren't drunk and we weren't children, but we were definitely foreign.

Six

"AMERIKA-JIN DESU KARA"

E*hisu* was the code name that Duncan and his team of programmers had chosen for our project. In the Japanese pantheon, Ebisu is one of the Seven Gods of Good Fortune who sail the seas in their dragon-prowed boat. He's the god of chance and the patron of workers and fishermen. Ebisu is also the name of a brand of beer. I found this interesting because the God I grew up with, a Methodist God with flashing eyes and a long white beard, would not have taken kindly to having a brand of beer named after him, or a software project either.

"Don't take the name of the Lord in vain," my mother used to scold me.

"But the Lord doesn't *have* a name," I would protest, showing early promise of that passion for the facts that makes me such a good technical writer.* "'God' is what he *is*, it isn't a *name*. And if he doesn't have a name, how can I take it in vain?" By this time my mother would be so angry that there was no chance of making my second point, which was that if saying, "Oh God!" made me feel better, then I hadn't said it "in vain."

---

* See? Boasting.

57

Ebisu didn't strike the HPJ office with a thunderbolt or afflict Duncan with boils, so I figured he didn't mind our taking his name in vain. Later, I would have cause to wonder about this, but for the time being things were going well. The enhancements were still infirm, but Tessa had taken pity on me and was letting me help her write a user manual.

I had also begun giving English lessons of a sort, thanks to an earnest e-mail message from Yoz.

Hi, Nano!
Miyuki-*san* and I want to have a good chance for English conversation periodically, and want to know more about European life style. And I want to train my English capability (hearing and speaking) more and more. Usual English class may be bore you, and I cannot have enough time for preparing and postparing for the class. So how about discussing or debating a certain theme once or twice a week for an hour? You are very busy and have few time for such a trivial thing, I know. But please ask my favor!
Best regards, Yoz.

Yes, Yoz needed to train his English capability more and more, but I couldn't help noticing that his spelling was perfect and that he used punctuation marks correctly. (The Japanese language doesn't require punctuation marks, so they have to be learned from scratch.) Furthermore, words like "periodically" and "debating" were part of his vocabulary, whereas all I could say in Japanese was, "Beer? It's cold."

Most of all, though, I was flattered by Yoz's belief that I was in touch with the European lifestyle. This is exactly the image that I try to create, and it hurts me that so few Americans fall for it. Obviously Yoz was impressed by my English boots and the photographs of French gargoyles that I'd pinned up in my cubicle, and I felt that his faith in me should be rewarded.

So, twice a week, Yoz and Miyuki and I met after work in the HPJ cafeteria. At first I assumed I'd make friends with them the way I had made friends with English people, in a process similar to climbing over a hedge without a ladder: prickly and time-consuming, but not impossible. You can't just walk up to a strange English person and start talking about your inner child. You have to say, "How do you do," talk about the weather for ten years, and *then* start talking about your inner child.

But there wasn't a hedge between me and the Tomodachi. There was a wall, a thick stone wall surrounded by a moat like the one around the Imperial Palace. Whole topics of conversation lay outside the wall: men, work, family relationships. When I was Miyuki's age, I had broken up with my fourth boyfriend, moved out of my fifth apartment, and traveled alone in Britain for three months. Miyuki had never traveled alone. Like most young Japanese women, she lived at home with her family, an arrangement that suited her. "I am happy every day to see my mother when I get home from work," she told me. I couldn't imagine being happy every day to see my family when I got home from work. I loved my parents, but I had "issues" with them. Didn't Miyuki have issues? Apparently not. No issues with work, either, and almost certainly (I wouldn't have dreamed of asking) no lovers. Not only couldn't I talk about my inner child, I'd have to keep quiet about my outer adult as well.

With Yoz it was possible to speak a bit more freely because Yoz and I had something significant in common. We were both misfits.

I'd figured out I was a misfit years before. I was working a summer job at Lockheed Missiles & Space Company in Sunnyvale, California, where both my father and my Uncle Hal were proud thirty-year employees. I had just completed my freshman year at college. I'd read Sartre, Yeats, and Auden, learned how trees get water from their roots to their leaves, and studied the history of Western civilization. My head was full of wonders, but all Lockheed cared about was how fast I could type.

All summer, I sat in a huge airline hangar of an office and typed weapon specifications on a manual typewriter. The walls were gray, the linoleum was gray, the desks were gray, the people were gray. The windows were frosted so you couldn't look outside and get distracted by a non-gray object, like a tree or something. The women were secretaries and wore round badges (hourly employees). The men were engineers and managers and wore rectangular badges (salaried employees). The engineers complained to me about their work, which gave them no satisfaction, and their wives, who were failing them on the same score. Adulthood, to hear them tell it, was one long succession of disappointing experiences.

They horrified me. If middle-class men couldn't manage better than this, what chance was I going to have? On breaks and at lunch, I holed up in the women's bathroom on a vinyl-covered sofa and read *The Lord of the Rings*. I tried to think of the engineers as endearing little Hobbits. Actually they were Ringwraiths, men who had given away their souls.

As often as not, when I completed a weapons spec for him, the engineer would say, "Thanks, but this is obsolete now," and toss my typing into the wastebasket. It was annoying but I didn't mind too much because I didn't want to help Lockheed make weapons. I had decided that despite my father and uncle, I hadn't been born to help the Lockheeds of this world make weapons or anything else. I was born for some purpose that only I was going to be able to discern, so the obvious course would be to work as little as possible until I had time to figure out what it was.

I was happy with this decision, but there's no denying that in America, where the Puritans moved because the English wouldn't let them work as many hours as they wanted to, an attitude like this makes you a weirdo.

But at least "weirdo" is a recognizable American identity. There probably isn't even a word for "weirdo" in Japan, a country where nothing seemed to exist outside the norm but a void of social oblivion. Americans are taught to prize the rugged individual. The Japanese prize the group, *dantai*, which offers protection in exchange for loyalty and shared responsibility. No one stands out, but no one is overlooked. "The nail that sticks up must be hammered down." All my Japanese colleagues gave the appearance of having been successfully hammered, with one exception: Yasuhiro Nakamura.

Yoz came from Osaka. He had this in common with several million other people, but apparently Osaka is not a good place to come from unless you never leave it. Yoz had left it. He was also the son of divorced parents. If you want to get married in Japan—and you do, even if you're gay, because it's your duty—you must not allow your parents to divorce. Your family's history will be researched by the parents of anyone you want to marry, and if they find divorce—well, to paraphrase Oscar Wilde, a passionate celibacy is all that you can look forward to.

So Yoz started out with two strikes against him. Then he made things worse for himself by doing seriously deviant things like growing a mustache and asking people to use his first name. (We foreigners did, but his Japanese colleagues went right on calling him Nakamura-*san*.) There didn't seem to be many Japanese weirdoes for him to hang out with, so he hung out with us Americans, which made him even weirder. He wasn't in the void of social oblivion, but it seemed to me that he was moving dangerously close to the outskirts.

He used our nicknames and adopted American slang. I asked him a question about Ebisu one day. "Hang on, Nano," he said, "I will check it out." He not only understood our culture, he began to practice it. Take irony, which seems to be unknown in Japan. One afternoon, Miyuki showed me a photograph of herself taken five years before. "Do you think I look much older now, Rhiannon-*san*?" she asked, eyes anxious in her flower-like face.

"Oh, yes," I said, "now you look positively ancient!" Miyuki stared at me, stricken. "*Jōdan deshita!* (It was a joke!)," I said quickly. "I was being ironic, Miyuki-*san*. Sometimes, in order to pay a compliment, we say the opposite of what we really mean. You see, if I thought you looked old, I would never say so, but since you don't . . ."

If you have to explain irony it sounds ridiculous, yet there are some of us for whom an ability to be ironic is practically a test of friendship. But I was never ironic with Miyuki again, or with any of my other colleagues, except for Yoz, who caught on to irony in a flash and rapidly progressed to sarcasm. He was the only Japanese person I met who didn't seem to be in perpetual pursuit of a Good Conduct prize. Everyone else—reliable George and good-natured Teddy, Stars the cosmos-gazer, Spats and the Imp, Mr. Goodwrench, Bobby, and my other colleagues—was diligent, disciplined, and chock-full of company spirit.

Take my boss, Ikeda. According to Tessa, he owned large chunks of Tokyo real estate and didn't need to earn a salary. In his position I would never have darkened an office door, but here was Ikeda at HPJ, being a marketing manager. Even "Easy Rider" Tsutsui, who rode a motorcycle, gave the impression that he did so only out of thoughtfulness, to leave more room on the road for lunatic taxi drivers.

HPJ had flex-time, but the Tomodachi were always at work by eight-thirty. HPJ had an eight-hour day, but almost everyone worked at least ten hours, and although HPJ had a five-day work week, most of the men came in on Saturdays.

And none of this nonsense about driving to work and parking in the company parking lot. There was a parking lot at the Takaido office, but it could accommodate only the cars of top executives. Everyone else commuted by train, an hour each way if they were lucky. (I can't remember whether Easy Rider rode his motorcycle to work. Perhaps he did, but I suspect there was a rule against it.) "Harpo" Sunaga, another of the lads, had a four-hour commute. I called him Harpo because in eighteen months, I never heard him speak. Of course, after two hours spent hanging on a strap to get to work, I wouldn't have felt like talking either.

The young women, "office ladies" like Miyuki, lived with their parents. Most of the young men lived in company dormitories. Each man was given a four-tatami-mat room: seventy-two square feet. No air conditioning. Shared bathrooms. A cafeteria. After five years in the dorm, the employee was expected to move out and get married, and HPJ helped pay the couple's rent. If the employee didn't get married, he had to leave the dorm anyway, but got no help with housing.

Not surprisingly, everyone got married. Everyone but weirdoes like Yoz, who had been in his dorm for too many years and was being asked (politely) to leave.

Put most Americans in a situation like that and we'd immediately start trying to improve it: work harder, work smarter, change jobs, move somewhere else. Few of these options were available to the lads. They had come to the company straight out of college and would stay in it until they retired, and they would be promoted according to seniority, no matter how hard or smart they worked. When they joined HPJ, they weren't hired for specific jobs with specific bosses. They could choose to work on the engineering side or on the financial side; all other decisions were made by the company. In 1985, the engineers' starting take-home pay was about four hundred dollars a month.

How would you feel if, in your early twenties, you had to live in a seventy-two-square-foot room, eat in cafeterias, spend two hours a day standing up in crowded trains, work fifty-plus hours a week, and get married when your company wanted you to? How would you feel if, once you joined a company, your future was set, with scant possibility of alteration? Would you brim over with enthusiasm, loyalty, *joie de vivre*?

My Japanese colleagues did. With what looked like a great deal less to be happy about than my American friends, they acted much happier. Unlike the Lockheed engineers, they didn't seem to be Ringwraiths. They laughed and joked and smiled and never complained, except for Yoz. And even Yoz didn't so much complain as comment.

Two possibilities exist. One is that the Tomodachi did manifest all the standard forms of unhappiness, only not in my presence.* The other is that they were genuinely happy. It was the latter possibility that haunted me, because I had so much more than they did—570 square feet full of stripped-pine furniture, plus the right to stay single for as long as I wanted—and I still wasn't happy.

Americans equate freedom with having choices. Thirty-one flavors of ice cream, all you can eat, call your own shots, make your own way. But we are also burdened with the responsibility of choosing and the need to accept the blame for choices made badly. When I lived in England, I met people who blamed "the class system"—probably with perfect justice—for failures that Americans would have blamed on themselves. Japan seemed to have gone one step further and created a system which offered so few choices that no occasion for blame could arise.

Which was better, I asked myself: to live safely and securely in a system like Japan's, relieved of the responsibility of making more than a few choices, or to walk the American tightrope over rocky ground? Or the European compromise: tightrope plus safety nets?

I had answered my question in the act of asking it. Like a good American, I was shopping around, convinced that I had

---

* Perhaps they attended the Festival of Abusive Language, an annual vent-fest, held just before midnight on New Year's Eve in Ashikaga, about 50 miles north of Tokyo. As festival-goers walk up a mountain toward the Saishoji Temple, they shriek curses into the sky. I would have loved to participate in this festival, but I didn't find out about it until after I'd left Japan.

Other festivals I wish I'd seen: the Bean-throwing festival; the Lantern festival (more than 3000 stone lanterns are lit in the precincts of the Kasuga Shrine in Nara); and the Demon festival, which according to the brochure consists of men disguised as devils going door-to-door and shouting, "Any good-for-nothing fellow here about?"

choices. ("I'll take a gallon of free-market capitalism and a pint of Scandinavian socialism, please.")

"Some day, when I'm rich," I said to Yoz, "I'll have . . ."

We were walking down my nameless lane toward Esta Shimizu. Yoz was carrying the "bilingual" VCR—capable of playing tapes from America—that he had just helped me buy. The cherry trees were covered in leafy green. I was tired, and in that state of edgy rubbed-the-wrong-wayness that shopping for stuff I don't understand (cars, anything with plugs) always produces in me.

I don't remember how I finished my sentence, but I remember Yoz's reply. "You think you may be rich some day?"

"Well, sure. I mean, it's a possibility. Don't you feel that way?"

"No," Yoz said. "I am *Japanese*. I know how much I will earn *this* year, *next* year, five *years* from now, when I retire. That's all I will *ever* have."

"Well . . . you have security, Yoz."

"Yes! Secure! But no—" With his empty hand, Yoz made a sharp, cramped gesture.

I stopped walking. "Yoz, if you want more, you should go for it. I believe that if you really want to, you can change your life—"

Yoz interrupted. "*Amerika-jin desu kara*," he said. *That's because you're American.* And he walked away from me, down the narrow lane between the crowded rows of houses.

Seven

DOES THIS TELEPHONE
GO TO KICHIJOJI?

When I think about living in Tokyo I see myself standing between the Colemans and the Marshalls, who are scowling at each other, while I gaze wistfully at the moated wall behind which the Tomodachi are laughing and joking and having a good time. There was a door in the moated wall and it was labeled *Nihongo*, the word for the Japanese language. If I wanted to get past the wall, I'd have to learn the language.

Private lessons were part of the Foreign Service Employee package, and at first I was cocky about my prospects. I'd been good at French in high school and college, so I expected to be good at Japanese. I can't carry a tune; I'm an indifferent cook; I'm useless at sports; but I do have a gift for arranging grammatical and syntactically effective sentences.

The first thing I learned from my Japanese teacher was that my gift for arranging sentences wasn't going to do me a blind bit of good. I would have to throw away everything I knew about how languages work and start again from scratch, like a one-year-old stringing sounds together.

In a Japanese sentence, my teacher explained, word order doesn't matter much, because the parts of speech are indicated by suffixes called "particles." So whereas we have to say, "I ride a bicycle to my office," or else get laughed at, the Japanese are allowed to go around saying things like, "The bicycle (particle) rides my office (particle) to me (particle)." The particles are small undistinguished monosyllables, hard to tell apart and easy to confuse with prepositions, so I was forever getting them muddled and saying things like, "I used to eat my boyfriend with ice cream," or, "A poodle owns my family."

The second thing I learned from my Japanese teacher was the principle of *yoin*. Literally, this means a reverberation, as when a bell is struck. Figuratively, it means that the Japanese prefer not to spell things out. Instead, you're supposed to utter a few well-chosen words and then let your sentence trail off, setting up echoes in the listener's mind that stimulate her imagination and allow her to complete your meaning for herself. This works in Japan because the people, with their common history and sense of unity, can often understand one another instinctively.

The way to be articulate in English is to be as precise as possible, but the opposite is true in Japanese. The truly cultured Japanese, I gathered, says virtually nothing at all, yet his fellow citizens not only understand him but marvel at how beautifully he speaks. But when I said, "A poodle . . ." and looked meaningfully at my teacher, she just sat there and waited for me to finish my sentence.

The third thing I learned from my Japanese teacher is the principle of *saho*, or etiquette. Although *saho* is not as strict as it used to be—in feudal times, Japan had the most demanding etiquette in the world, with carefully prescribed ways of sleeping, walking, and even sitting—every person is still ranked in a hierarchical system and you must pitch your level of speech accordingly. Before you can say anything, you must decide whether the person you're addressing is your inferior, your equal, or your superior.

Americans do make similar distinctions. We might say, "Grab a chair" to a friend, but to a visiting cleric we'd say, "Please have a seat." It's also true that in the U.S., as in Japan, men tend to use blunter, coarser language than women. But we do this without thinking about it because we believe that we're a classless society in which all persons are created equal and no one is any better than anyone else. I recognized that at home I used different levels of speech in different situations, but in Japan I found myself rebelling against the need to make these distinctions explicit.

"It is strange, Rhiannon-*san*," said my teacher, when I tried to explain, haltingly, that I preferred to just be nice to everyone. "All my American students have trouble with this, but my English students understand the Japanese way." Not strange at all. In Britain, the same kind of ranking is achieved through accents that give away the speaker's social class.

When you're trying to speak French, you can construct an English sentence in your head, substitute French words, tweak the sentence a bit, and you're ready to go. "I am giving you the book"—"*Je vous donne le livre*." The only difficulty is remembering whether "book" is feminine or masculine. But suppose you're in Japan and you want to say "I am giving you the book" to a man named Mr. Kubo. Here's the process you have to go through:

"I"	Omit the subject if it can be inferred from context. Mr. Kubo can see who's giving him the book. You don't want to insult him with too much specificity. If you decide to say "I" anyway, use the standard form unless it's a formal occasion, followed by *wa* (particle indicating subject of sentence). Or maybe *ga*,

according to a rule that probably makes perfect sense but that I never understood.*

"am giving"   Use one of three verbs for "give" depending on whether Mr. Kubo is your inferior, your equal, or your superior. Take into consideration his sex and yours, his age and yours—men outrank women; age outranks youth—his job and yours, and anything else that affects your status *vis-à-vis* one another. Then decide whether to use the plain form or the polite form of the verb. If you're female, you should use the polite form unless Mr. Kubo is so inferior he's beneath contempt. (In which case, why are you giving him a book?)

"you"   Kubo-*san* is not a family member, so "you" is too intimate. Say his surname. Yes, even though you're looking at him. And don't forget the *san*. Then say *ni* (particle indicating indirect object.)

"the"   Omit. There are no articles in Japanese.

"book"   Follow it with *o* (particle indicating the object of an action).

Finally, rearrange the sentence as follows: subject + indirect object + direct object + verb. That's the preferred order for a sentence in Japanese. (Usually.) Now, put it all together: "I *wa* Kubo-*san ni* book *o* give."

Okay! (In Japanese, *Hai dōzo!*) Let's move on to a slightly more difficult sentence from *The Story of Philosophy* by Will Durant:

---

* I've just looked it up in my Japanese grammar book. *Wa* indicates the topic of the sentence and *ga* indicates the subject. So now you know.

It is a common delusion that the great periods of culture have been ages of hereditary aristocracy: on the contrary, the efflorescent periods of Pericles and the Medici and Elizabeth and the Romantic age were nourished with the wealth of a rising bourgeoisie; and the creative work in literature and art was done not by aristocratic families but by the offspring of the middle class,—by such men as Socrates, who was the son of a midwife, and Voltaire, who was the son of an attorney, and Shakespeare, who was the son of a butcher.

No problem! Since the Japanese prefer not to be specific, we can reduce this entire sentence to, "Middle class *wa* good culture *o* give." Although it's too bad they have to miss the part about Shakespeare being the son of a butcher.

So it's really very easy and I can't imagine now why I made such a fuss about it. Although you do run into problems when you have to count something. For example, in Japanese, the word "seven" is *nana*. (Unless it's *shichi*. There are two ways to say "seven" and two ways to say "four.") But if you're counting, say, tickets, seven is *nana-mai*; *mai* is the counter for thin flat things. If you're counting beer in bottles, seven is *nana-hon*; *hon* is the counter for long slender things. If the beer's in glasses, seven is *nana-hai* (liquid things in cups or glasses), but once the glasses are empty, seven is *nana-ko* (empty glasses or bowls).

There are counters for lessons, books, pages, boats, large electrical appliances, floors of a building, overnight stays, doses of medicine, pairs of footgear, birds, cats, people, and heads of cattle. There are more than a hundred different counters, but don't worry. As a foreigner, you're only expected to master about a dozen.

When I first moved to Japan, I took an optimistic view of the language barrier. "I have decided," I wrote home, "that there's a great deal to be said for moving through life illiterate and uncomprehending. Information is thrust upon me—in billboards, shop signs, headlines—but it's all in little pictures and I can't read it. The conversations I overhear are a stream of meaningless syllables. For the first time in my life, I can go into the outside world and still hear myself think. It's curiously refreshing."

But that was when I was staying at the Century Hyatt Hotel, calling Room Service every morning for my cornflakes and traveling to and from work in taxis. Once I'd moved into an apartment and started buying my own cornflakes, it was no longer refreshing to be illiterate. I got tired of speaking simple English so my Japanese colleagues could understand me. I got tired of feeling guilty because they *had* to understand me, owing to my inability to understand them. I got tired of feeling like a fool.

Scene 1: I'm standing in a minuscule grocery store near Nishi Eifuku station, looking at a clear plastic bag filled with white granules. It's either sugar or salt, but which? The bag has red writing on it, but the writing is in Japanese. I don't know the words for sugar or salt. I want to buy sugar for my coffee, a word I do know, so I take the bag up to the counter. Holding the bag up so the shopkeeper can see it, I ask, "*Kō-hī?*" (Rhymes with "no tea.")

His face clouds. (Is this foreigner insane?) "*Iie,*" he says, "*kō-hī janai.* (No, that isn't coffee.)"

I mime spooning sugar into a cup. I try to do this intelligently, but in fact it's difficult to look intelligent when you're miming.

The shopkeeper's face clears. (Not insane, just monolingual.) He takes the bag from me, returns it to the shelf, and brings me a similar bag labeled in blue. "*Satō desu,*" he says. ("This is sugar.")

Scene 2: I'm in Meidamae station on what I hope is the right platform, watching a train come in. Is it the train to Kichijoji? I've learned how to say, "Does this train go to . . ." so

I turn to the man next to me and ask, "*Kono denwa wa, Kichijoji ni ikimasu ka?*"

"*Hai,*" he responds courteously, "*ikimasu yo.* (Yes, it does.)" I board the train and bask in my small success until I remember that the word for train is *densha,* not *denwa.* What I asked the nice man was, "Does this telephone go to Kichijoji?"

Challenged by a language I couldn't read, write, or speak, and condemned to utter wincing sentence fragments and mime idiotically instead of expressing myself in full polysyllabic splendor, I beat up on Japanese because it made me feel inferior. "What can you do with a language," I wrote home, "in which 'eleven o'clock on November eleventh' emerges as *jū-ichi-ji jū-ichi-gatsu jū-ichi-nichi?*"

That I learned any Japanese at all is due to my teacher, Yamaguchi-*sensei.** Fortyish, gracious, sincere, and eager, with a round face and a sweet smile, she labored for eighteen months to bring me from the darkness into the light, or at least to teach me the difference between "train" and "telephone." The odds were against her, as I revealed in my letters home.

August, 1985: "My teacher, Mrs. Yamaguchi, now has me taking two classes a week instead of one. Apparently I'm her star pupil and she has great hopes for me. This is amazing, since I generally memorize the entire lesson one hour before the class."

November, 1985: "I am having a hard time believing that any language can be as different from English as Japanese seems to be. After seven months of study I can barely utter a sentence."

January, 1986: "My Japanese is still minimal. The more I learn, the less I seem able to say. A few months ago I could at least tell you what time it was. Then I started learning verb tenses in both plain and polite forms and now I can barely remember how to count to five. My teacher, once convinced that

---

* *Sensei* is a special honorific used for teachers. The Japanese think they're important.

she was assisting in the enlightenment of a prodigy, now says it's all right to go slowly. The inscrutable East has met the untutorable West, and it's winning."

March, 1986: "I have finally learned one of the three writing systems, *hiragana*, which means I'm at about the same level as a Japanese four-year-old. Now I have to memorize a second set of symbols, *katakana*. Then all I need to do is learn a few thousand *kanji* characters and I'll be able to read a newspaper."

The *kana* characters, *hiragana* and *katakana*, are syllabaries, which means that each character represents one vowel or syllable (*ka, ki, ku, ke, ko*, etc.). *Hiragana* are used to write simple words, conjugations at the end of verbs, and particles. *Katakana*—the same syllables and vowels, but with different symbols—are used to write foreign words.*

Kanji are the Chinese pictorial characters that the Japanese adopted from the Chinese in the fourth century A.D. A *kanji* character can require as many as forty separate strokes of the pen to write, and each stroke must be made in the correct order and direction. It takes Japanese children about eleven years to learn the 1850 *kanji* that are required for literacy, which works out at a bit more than 168 *kanji* a year. Most educated Japanese learn an additional 650 to 1000 characters. Americans should be chastened to learn that since 1970, despite using the most difficult system of writing, Japan has achieved the world's highest literacy rate: 99+%.

In eighteen months, I learned two *kanji: yama* and *guchi*. I learned them not because they formed my Japanese teacher's name—that was a happy coincidence—but because they were simple: *Guchi*, mouth, is a square box; *Yama*, mountain, looks like a three-pronged fork without a handle. I could memorize

---

* There are about 100 *kana* characters. I say "about" because my reference books give different amounts: some say 46, some say 48, others say 52. Sources are equally disputatious about the total number of *kanji* available to the Japanese, with figures ranging from 10,000 to 50,000.

anything in words, even Japanese words. Given time, I thought I could master the grammar. But when it came to *kanji*, I put my hands up and surrendered. I would never be able to read Japanese. I couldn't see myself memorizing even one hundred characters, let alone 1850. This meant being stuck forever on my side of the moated wall, for I'd have known, even if Yoz hadn't kept telling me, that *kanji* were one of the keys to his culture.

"I think this is why we *Japanese* are so *good* at pattern recognizing," he said. "And also the *kanji* are *beautiful*. They contain the hidden *meanings*, and *often* they explain themselves."

"What do you mean, they explain themselves?"

"Look, Nano." He wrote several *kanji* on a sheet of paper. "This first one is '*onna*,' woman. And these are '*dorei*,' slave. See how 'slave' contains the *kanji* for 'woman'?"

Not the happiest example he could have chosen. Other examples are *hyōga*, "glacier," which contains the *kanji* for "ice" and "river," and *kokogaku*, "archeology," which contains the *kanji* for "study," "antiquity," and "science."

The Japanese take pride in the complexity of their language. Whenever I complained about *nihongo* being *muzukashii* (difficult), my colleagues smiled. They could read *hiragana*, *katakana*, thousands of *kanji*, and the English alphabet. The men could also read programming languages. All I could read was the alphabet.

As for the *kana* characters, *hiragana* and *katakana*, as soon as I had memorized them, I began to forget them. Either I've got no gift for pattern recognizing or I didn't try hard enough. The Colemans and the Marshalls picked up the *kana* characters without difficulty, and learned lots of *kanji* as well.

Because I didn't retain the *kana* characters, I couldn't read menus, on which foreign foods are labeled in *katakana*, making it easy to order things like pizza and cappuccino. And shop signs were meaningless. In the absence of a sidewalk or window display, I couldn't tell whether the shop in question sold blowfish, bunion pads, or bicycle tires.

In fact, I was able to use the *kana* characters only once. Traveling with English friends, I was struck by a bad headache. None of us had any aspirin. The shop windows were covered with the usual colorful riot of incomprehensible characters, but as I gazed at them, three symbols suddenly attached themselves to pronunciation and then made the further leap to meaning.

"*Ku, su, ri,*" I read. "*Kusuri.* Hey, that means drugs!" So I went in and mimed having a headache because I didn't know the word for aspirin, and the pharmacist smiled sympathetically at me and said, "You wish to buy some aspirin?"

It was all downhill from there, although my miming continued to improve. Only my liking for Yamaguchi-*sensei* kept me at it, trying to figure out the difference between *wa* and *ga*, memorizing new verb tenses—the conditional, the volitional, the passive, the causative, the potential, the imperative—and taking pages of diligent notes in a green binder I bought for the purpose. Like many Japanese products, the binder has English words on it. The front cover advises, in big white letters —

do it
your
self!

But I didn't do it myself. To the extent that I did it at all, my teacher gets the credit.

Dōmo arigatō gozaimashita, Yamaguchi-sensei. Thank you very much.

Eight

○

THE MOON IN THE WATER

Chinese traders landed in Kyūshū, the southernmost of Japan's three main islands, in the second century B.C. They described the people they found as farmers and fishermen, divided into tribes that were stratified according to classes and ruled by male or female chieftains who were also regarded as priests. The religion of these people, still practiced in Japan, is now called Shinto, "the way of the gods." Wherever the early Japanese looked in nature, they saw gods smiling back at them: gods in the mountains, gods in the trees, gods in the rivers, gods in the rocks.

The gods of Shinto don't trade in ethical systems, prohibitions, or commandments. Neither does Buddhism, introduced from China in the sixth century. There are 100,000-plus Shinto shrines in Japan and about 77,000 Buddhist temples. Most Japanese today practice bits of both religions, but no God tells them how to live or threatens to punish them if they stray.

I asked myself how this system could have produced the conscientious, squeaky-clean, scrupulously well-behaved men and women I kept meeting. If you know you won't go to hell for doing bad things, then why not do bad things?

When I asked Miyuki to explain her culture to me, she said, "Rhiannon-*san*, we are a small mountainous country with few natural resources."* I posed the same question to Mrs. Yamaguchi. "We are a small mountainous country with few natural resources." The Imp? "We are a small mountainous country with few natural resources." You could put this question to a Japanese street-sweeper and he would answer, "We are a small mountainous country with few natural resources." Every schoolchild in Japan is required to memorize this sentence on the off-chance that someday he'll meet an inquisitive foreigner.

I hoped that Yoz, the outsider, might give me a different answer. He did. He pronounced "mountainous" as "moun-*tane-ee-ous.*"

"Yes, yes, I know," I said. "Small islands sitting on the geological equivalent of Jello, or riding the back of a catfish if you prefer. Lots of typhoons and fires so nothing is permanent. Scarce arable land. No oil. You rely on imports for most of your energy, so you have to cooperate and work hard to make things that people want to buy. But how come you're so good at it?"

Yoz lit a cigarette and inhaled. "If an *American* child does something *bad* in school, *who* gets punished?"

"Well, he does, of course."

"*Ah sō desu.* In Japan, the whole *class* gets punished."

I gaped at him. "For something one kid does? But that's not fair!"

"Fair," Yoz said, blowing the word away like smoke.

In the U.S., it's you against the teacher, against the boss, against the system. You can disobey all you want as long as you're prepared to take the consequences. And some people will admire you: rebel, individualist, challenger of authority. In

---

* Only about sixteen percent of Japanese land can be cultivated, and human settlement is confined to about three percent, in a country that is roughly the size of California.

Japan, everyone takes the consequences and no one admires you. And you never misbehave again.

Were the Japanese right? When a child disrupts a class doesn't everyone suffer, even though she's the only one who gets punished? When a man robs and kills don't we all suffer, even if he's the only one who goes to jail? Is it better to teach this lesson early, by punishing everyone, by giving children no incentive ever to be bad again?

But rebellion isn't always bad, I reminded myself. And what else is lost, besides bad behavior, when people are raised to put the group first?

"How did you come to be this way?" I asked Yoz.

"You must *read* Japanese *history*."

"Oh, well . . . couldn't you just, like, tell me?"

"For the answer to be *complete*, you must have very many hours. I *think* you won't have time enough to listen."

So I read Japanese history. Like the history of every other country I've studied, it seemed to consist primarily of men fighting each other, a subject that bores me to tears, no matter how entertaining Hollywood tries to make it. (The female chieftains encountered by the Chinese traders don't seem to have lasted long.) But I began to see what Yoz meant. Men plotted, ambushed, stabbed, shot, and disemboweled their way through the centuries; peasants gained, lost, and regained land; the *samurai* wielded and were divested of their swords; the capital moved from Nara to Kyoto to Kamakura to Tokyo; wars were fought with China, Russia, the United States; the *shogun* (military regents) and the *daimyō* (feudal lords) gave way to a constitution and a Diet patterned after the English parliament. So many changes, and yet—

The moon in the water;
Broken and broken again,
Still it is there.

—Choshu

From the beginning there is an attachment to hierarchy. It's there in the second century B.C., in the sharply defined classes noted by the Chinese, and it has survived. As Ruth Benedict noted in her landmark book about Japan, *The Chrysanthemum and the Sword*, on the day that Pearl Harbor was attacked, Japanese envoys delivered a message to the U.S. Secretary of State, stating that the Japanese government wanted each nation to find "its proper place" in the world. One learns the importance of one's proper place by means of the family, where, as Benedict says, the wife bows to her husband, the child bows to his father, younger brothers bow to elder brothers, and sisters bow to all their brothers. Men used to find their proper place in the service of feudal lords. Today, they slot themselves into hierarchies at Honda, Matsushita, Seiko, or Hewlett-Packard Japan. A Japanese used to be born into his place; now he has to compete for it. But the hierarchy persists.

So does a sense of being special; not superior to other nations, necessarily, but set apart. British history begins with a series of invasions: Celts, Anglo-Saxons, Vikings, Romans, Normans. But no one invaded Japan. The Mongols under Kublai Khan tried to, in 1274 and 1281. After weeks of fierce battles, they were finally driven away by bad weather, including a typhoon that the Japanese called the *kamikaze* ("divine wind").

In 1543, ships brought Portuguese traders and Jesuit priests. This was Japan's first encounter with Europeans. The priests won almost half a million converts. Guns, which the Japanese had never seen before, won even more. In turn, the Japanese won the respect of their foreign visitors. According to Alessandro Valignano, one of the priests, even the peasants were so well brought up that they seemed to have been trained at court. The people were intelligent, he noted, and the children quick to grasp their lessons.

"Let a stranger in, and he will drive you out of your own home." Toward the end of the century, Japan's military rulers began to see truth in that proverb. The guns could stay, but the missionaries had to go. Japanese Christians were told to renounce God or die. Most chose to die. In 1637, an imperial edict declared that anyone who tried to leave Japan, and all Japanese returning from foreign countries, would be put to death. Imagine the heartbreak of the Japanese who were stranded forever in foreign lands.

For almost two hundred years, Japan disappeared from every history except her own. The Japanese had only themselves, and they found themselves sufficient. The country enjoyed uninterrupted peace and growing prosperity. Thanks in part to a sensible system whereby a couple could adopt a son and heir so they didn't have to keep "trying for a boy," the population remained relatively steady and the standard of living rose for almost everyone. Artists painted, wove, wrote haiku, erected and decorated buildings, fashioned porcelain, lacquerware, brocades. An urban merchant class developed with its own amusement quarters and its own art, *ukiyo-e*, "pictures of the fleeting world." From *ukiyo-e* came multicolored wood-block prints, puppet theater, *kabuki*, and the professional female entertainers now called *geisha*.

Crowded together in their beautiful "moun-*tane*-ee-ous" country, given little room to maneuver by an oppressive feudal system, the Japanese learned how to cooperate with one another and live harmoniously in the world that had been given to them by their gods.

The West was not impressed. From the West's point of view, Japan had fallen behind: no trains, no telegraph poles, no dark satanic mills. What was worse, what was unforgivable, was that the Japanese refused to buy things that the West wanted to sell. They were ignoring the central principle of the modern age: *Thou shalt consume.*

In 1853, by way of a gentle hint, the United States sent Commodore Perry with half the U.S. Navy. "Our cannons are bigger than your cannons," was the message. Our cannons *were* bigger, so the Japanese negotiated a treaty with the U.S. and subsequent treaties with European countries. All these treaties were unequal, giving far more advantages to the West than to Japan.

The Japanese reacted variously to the end of their dream-like isolation. Popular movements arose, adopting colorful mottoes such as "Restore the emperor and expel the barbarians" and "Rich country, strong military."

In 1868, the Shogunate, which had been established in 1185 by Yoritomo Minamoto, was overthrown by a coalition of *daimyō*, the feudal lords, who seized control of the court and announced the resumption of direct imperial rule. This would have been remarkable if it had happened, for the emperors of Japan, although greatly revered, had seldom exercised real power. (Perhaps that's why they were revered.) In the fifteenth century, some emperors were so poor that they eked out a living by selling samples of their calligraphy. But in 1868 the emperor was a fifteen-year-old boy. Everything was done in his name, but he didn't run the show.

During the Meiji Restoration, as it came to be called, the new rulers of Japan remade the government and economy along European lines. They moved the emperor and the capital to Edo and renamed it Tokyo ("eastern capital"). After studying examples from many nations, they issued a constitution in 1889, which created the Diet. It also made official what everyone had known for centuries: that the emperor was a divinely descended focus for the nation's identity and pride, but not an actual ruler.

Children began singing "The Civilization Ball Song." With each bounce of the ball, they named one of the ten desirable Western things: schools, gas lamps, steam-engines, horse-drawn carriages, newspapers, steamboats, cameras, lightning rods, telegraphs, and a postal service.

The Japanese got trains, telegraph poles, and dark satanic mills, but also universal education and limited male suffrage.* The peasants got the land they'd been living on. The old feudal domains were replaced by prefectures, administered by officials from the central government. The *samurai*, the hereditary class of warriors, were told to hang up their swords. Some of them tried to rebel, but unsuccessfully. Japan was becoming a meritocracy.

So from the beginning there was also an inclination to see the new, the strange, the foreign, and think: "*Sugoi desu ne*— roughly, "Hey, this is great—How can we adapt this and make it ours?" Christianity couldn't be borrowed because its One God Only wouldn't live in harmony with the gods in the mountains and the rocks and the trees. But Buddhism and Confucianism were borrowed from China. The Chinese characters (*kanji*) were cobbled together with spoken Japanese, a patch job that had to be supplemented by *hiragana* and *katakana*. Sure of their identity, their common descent from the Goddess of Light, their ties to the emperor and to each other, the people of Japan could remake themselves again and again and yet remain uniquely Japanese.

So far, so good, I thought, skimming through *The Chrysanthemum and the Sword*. Living in a hierarchy has its advantages. Perhaps I should recommend it to the folks back home. I turned the page and began to read Benedict's "Schematic Table of Japanese Obligations and their Reciprocals," a table that occupies a full page of very small type. It begins with *on*, the "obligations passively incurred." *On* is received first of all from the emperor and then from one's parents, teachers, employers, and others (one's *on jin* or "*on* men"). *On* can never be repaid, but one must nevertheless spend a lifetime trying by means of

---

* Japanese women didn't get the vote until after World War II, in an amendment to the constitution that was drafted by General MacArthur's staff.

chu (duty to the emperor, the law, and Japan), *ko* (duty to one's parents and ancestors), and *nimmu* (duty to one's work). Collectively, these repayments are called *gimu*.

I shrugged my shoulders, which were feeling cramped. I read on, and learned that *gimu* is nothing compared with *giri*, a uniquely Japanese concept, unlike *chu* and *ko*, which were borrowed from China. *Gimu* is the attempt to repay the debts you were born with, but *giri* is what you accumulate as you move through life: duties to your spouse's family, to nieces and nephews, to colleagues, etc.

If you do a favor for an acquaintance or a stranger, you may "make him wear an *on*" that he will never be able to repay with *giri*, and he may resent it bitterly. What we might interpret as a refusal to get involved or to help another person may be, in Japan, the ultimate sign of consideration. "How unfortunate, fellow-citizen, that you are lying in the street, run over by a taxi driver! From the angle at which your left leg is sticking up, I deduce that it is broken in at least one place. No doubt you are in pain and would like to be comforted. However, if I came to your assistance, I would be putting an *on* on you, for I am a complete stranger whom you will never see again. Therefore I will show you the courtesy of pretending that I don't hear your screams of agony, and go on my way."

But wait (I turned another page): you wouldn't be screaming in agony, because in addition to what Benedict calls "*giri*-to-the-world," there's "*giri*-to-one's-name," or the duty to maintain a good reputation. This concept, also unique to the Japanese, entails the careful observance of etiquette; an avoidance of competition (too shameful for the losers); a hypersensitivity to slights and insults; and a stoical acceptance of discomfort, disaster, and pain. If your superior officer orders you to fly your airplane into the deck of an aircraft carrier, you obey. In the agonies of childbirth, you maintain a dignified silence. Although your colleagues smoke like chimneys and fluorescent lights

make your eyes ache, you would never dream of complaining
. . . Oops.

Giri-to-one's-name also requires that you accept your station in life rather than striving to "get ahead" and improve your
situation. Equality is not important; individual achievement is
not important. What *is* important is finding your proper place
and staying there. This builds *wa*, harmony or balance, which
derives from the Shinto principle that people must maintain
peaceful relations amongst themselves and with nature.

I set the book down and rubbed my aching shoulders. There
was not going to be any point in recommending a hierarchical
system to the folks at home.

I heard Yoz saying "*Amerika-jin desu kara* . . . that's because you're an American" as he walked away from me down
my lane. All around him I saw the shadowy figures of his ancestors, thousands of them, and every one Japanese, all speaking the same language and sharing the same culture: business-
men, artisans, fishermen, farmwives, dressed in suits, in kimonos, in simple robes, ending with the Goddess of Light herself,
robed and shining. Yoz was tied to each of them and to every
other Japanese, held securely in a dense net of connections, protected alike from rising and falling.

I pictured my own ancestors and saw the Neills (Irish) blam-
ing the Barnes (English) for centuries of oppression. The Barnes
protested that as agricultural laborers—peasants—they'd been
plenty oppressed themselves. The Roberts chimed in, pointing
out that it hadn't been any picnic down those Welsh coal-mines
either, boyo. The Burkhardts and the Boohers said "What about
the treaty of Versailles, then?" but they said it in German so no
one understood them, and the Paines muttered "Bloody Jerries"
under their breath. My father's great-grandfather, Samuel Gold,
born in Edinburgh, raised a plaintive voice, asking whether I
thought he was Scottish, Jewish, or both? I couldn't answer
him. Past a few generations, I don't know who any of my an-

cestors were, what countries they came from, what flags they fought under, what languages they spoke, what allegiances they held. I don't feel tied in a dense net of connections, securely held and protected. I've always known that I'm on my own.

Nine

BIKE RIDE TO MITAKA

Travel writers tend to describe Tokyo in similar terms. First they gave you the bad news. Here's Frances FitzGerald writing in *Esquire*, July 1983:

> From the raised expressways crossing the city Tokyo looks like a nightmare of megalopolis . . . The sea and the mountains are too far away to orient it, and the rivers too shallow to be more than interruptions in the sprawl of concrete . . . Tokyo is everywhere a jumble of the old and the new, of factories and office buildings and residential streets . . . Driving for an hour across Tokyo, one seems to get nowhere at all.

And here's Thomas A. Sancton in the May 5, 1986 issue of *Time* magazine:

> To outsiders Tokyo is an urban nightmare: skyscrapers thrown up helter-skelter against a backdrop of chemical haze . . . subways so crowded that white-gloved "pushers"

are required to cram riders in; towering residential blocks in which whole families inhabit the space of two-car garages; garish neon jungles that blink like electronic votive candles to the modern-day god of consumerism.

Sancton's article includes a quotation from designer Yohji Yamamoto:

> It is a city without concept. There is no fixed landscape. The scenery leaves no impression. If I were asked to paint a picture of Tokyo, I suppose I would make a sad, vague study of square buildings standing tall against the fog.

You get the picture: traffic snarling through nameless streets in the perpetual shadow of anonymous buildings packed with people, while shallow rivers trickle toward the distant sea under a sky full of chemicals. And it is certainly true that Tokyo is like that.

In 1986, Greater Tokyo consisted of twenty-three wards, twenty-six sub-cities, fifteen towns and villages, and several islands. (I specify the year because it's possible that Tokyo has swallowed up even more towns and cities since I lived there.) Central Tokyo alone covered 930 square miles and had a population of about twelve million people. Los Angeles had half as many square miles and a population of under four million; London had 600-odd square miles and a population of about seven million. So Tokyo had five million more people than London. *Five million more.*

Tokyo has no center. There's no such thing as "downtown Tokyo." There's no such thing as "downtown London" either, but you can orient yourself by the Thames, by parks and landmarks: you're near Kew Gardens, or between St. Paul's and the Tower, or on the South Bank. There's nothing to orient yourself by in Tokyo: few parks (London has more than twenty times as

much parkland), no hills or mountains, no distinguished buildings or monuments—not even the emperor's residence, surely
the only palace in the world to be made out of ferroconcrete.

In fact, notes FitzGerald, Tokyo has no public architecture
at all, which is probably a blessing because the architecture that
exists is hideous beyond belief. Draw a tall rectangle with
squares in it. Paint it gray. Draw tens of thousands of them.
Around them, draw thickets of poles bearing dense strands of
electricity and telephone cables. Cover the ground with millions of dots (the people). That's Tokyo.

The city's old name was *Edo*, meaning estuary. A network
of waterways converged there. I don't know what happened to
the waterways. An earthquake leveled the city in 1923 and it
had a scant twenty years to rebuild before American bombs flat-
tened it again. Almost everything you see was built in the last
fifty years; most of the buildings, including the Imperial Palace, are younger than I am. It is not an easy place in which to
feel the presence of the past.

It is also not an easy place in which to be alone. There are
people everywhere, dozens of them in the tiny streets of my
neighborhood, thousands of them on the bigger thoroughfares,
competing for space with the city's four million-plus registered
motor vehicles. Most commuter trains run at double the intended
occupancy, which means that half the people on board lack even
a strap to hold. When occupancy reaches two hundred fifty percent instead of the usual two hundred percent, you can't even
move your hands.

Shinjuku station is the most used—several million people
daily—but every few months I would brave it for a particular
purpose. I would walk ten minutes from my apartment to Nishi
Eifuku station, take the Inokashira Line to Meidamae, change
to the Keio Line, get off at Shinjuku, walk twenty minutes to
Kinokuniya Bookstore, and mount five flights of stairs to the
gaijin book department.

I didn't usually buy books, I just wanted to hang out with them for a while; but one Saturday afternoon I paid for three, which were duly wrapped in white paper and tied up with string. In Shinjuku station, I boarded the train for Meidamae, found a place to stand, and stuck my new books on the floor between my feet. As more people boarded, I was pushed farther down the train. Meanwhile the package got edged out from between my feet and propelled along the floor toward the opposite end of the car.

We left Shinjuku and made the usual stops at Hatsudai, Hatagaya, Sasazuka, Daitabashi. People got off. People got on. I gazed hopelessly in the direction my books had gone. They were in another compartment by now, I figured. Possibly in another train.

We pulled into Meidamae, our numbers somewhat reduced. As I pushed my way toward the door, wondering darkly how anyone could bear to live in a hell-hole like Tokyo, someone touched my arm. Over heads in the distance, a familiar package burst into view. In silence, my books were passed from hand to hand over people's heads down the full length of the compartment until they reached the passenger next to me. "*Onegaishimasu*," he said—a handy expression that can mean "please" or "excuse me" or, in this context, "allow me"—and gave me my package.

The good news about Tokyo is her people. All the travel writers get around to that, after they've finished going on about garish neon jungles and sad buildings in the fog. You would think that people who live in a place described as "a nightmare of megalopolis" would be mercenary cut-throats, especially if they had to pronounce "megalopolis" very often. But you'd be wrong. Tokyo is one of the safest places on earth. My package would have been returned to me down the length of that train if it had consisted of rubies wrapped in clear plastic and labeled in Japanese, "Worth more money than a square foot of land on the Ginza."

Unlike us Americans, the Japanese do not go in for rob-
bing, raping, and killing one another in a big way.* They don't
have the Right to Bear Arms so beloved by the National Rifle
Association, but they endure this misfortune with equanimity.
Perhaps they prefer to keep their children safe. Of all the sights
I saw in Japan—and I'm including a Shinto ceremony, public
bathing in the nude, and a snack food made out of squid—the
most foreign sight was that of small children traveling alone by
train.

"When they start first grade," explained Christine Yamada,
a secretary who joined the SPN group in August, "they are old
enough to go to school alone."

"At six years old?"

"Oh, you don't realize it, but every adult on the train is
looking out for that child, and if he seems lost or frightened,
some adult will take care of him and make sure he gets where
he needs to be."

In Tokyo, a city of twelve million people, you can rely on
the kindness of strangers. You can entrust your children to the
kindness of strangers. Think what it would be like to live like
that.

"Never before in my life have I felt so safe," I wrote home.
"It's not just that there's so little crime; it's more subtle than
that: there's no feeling of menace or hostility among the people.
Little girls of seven and eight wheel around the city on bicycles.
If you drop a yen-stuffed wallet, someone will pick it up and
turn it in to the police station. If you leave your bike unlocked
outside Tokyu *depāto*, it will be there when you get back. The
only thing that seems to get ripped off is umbrellas, and I forgot
to bring one so I've got nothing to worry about."

---

* In 1984, the year before I moved to Tokyo, New York City had
  about eleven times as many murders, twenty-three times as many
  rapes, and two hundred times as many robberies.

Kōban (police boxes) are partly accountable for the safety of Japan's streets. Established by the Tokugawa Shogunate in 1628, they were intended to offer protection from renegade *samurai* who habitually used commoners for sword practice. (By law, a *samurai* could kill a commoner for bad behavior, with the *samurai* deciding what constituted "bad." Nose-blowing would definitely have counted.) There are *kōban* everywhere; the nearest one to the House of Clear Water was outside Nishi Eifuku station, about ten minutes away. In theory, the police watch over their neighborhoods; in practice, they spend a lot of time helping people find addresses.

Her people make the city work. If they weren't thrilled to be living in Tokyo (and most of them are), if they weren't perfectly well-behaved and law-abiding, you couldn't bear to be there. As it is, you've got the best of both worlds: the buzz that comes from big-city living in proximity to millions of people, and a complete absence of fear.

The buzz in Tokyo is almost audible, a high-energy hum that sizzles like electricity through the veins of the susceptible. Add the excitement of meeting challenges, of learning one's way around a completely new place, and even a sedentary house-hermit like me (motto: "I get all the exercise I need from lifting books") gets zapped into action.

One Saturday evening I'd been invited to the Colemans' for dinner. My usual way of getting to their apartment was to take the train to Kichijoji, change to the Chuo line, take the train to Mitaka, and then walk the rest of the way. As I locked my metal door, I decided on impulse to ride my bicycle instead. I knew that the Inokashira Dōri ran all the way to Mitaka, so I extemporized a seat-of-the-pants navigation system that consisted of riding down the I.D. until I'd gone through Kichijoji, and then asking people the way to Mitaka station. Once I'd found the station, I simply rode the rest of the route. My trip took about ninety minutes.

Paul and Tessa were amazed that I'd done something so spontaneous, so mettlesome, so out of character. When it started to drizzle as we ate dessert, they urged me to stay the night, but I said no. This might be the only chance I would ever have to ride a bicycle alone at night through a huge city. I intended to take it.

I set off just before eleven o'clock. The drizzle turned to rain. Cars and trucks went howling down the Inokashira Dōri. A few men reeled along the sidewalks, drunk but harmless, on their way home from office parties. Water dripped through my hair. My wheels splashed through puddles. The neon signs of Mitaka and Kichijoji blurred and swam in the damp air. I felt exhilarated, wild and free. I was out at night alone and I wasn't being foolish or reckless or "asking for trouble." There were no bad parts of town, no places I had to stay out of, no times of day when I had to be locked up at home. Tokyo didn't belong to men who would hurt me if I wasn't careful, if I strayed onto their turf, if I went to the wrong place at the wrong time. Tokyo belonged to me, all 930 square miles of it.

SUMMER

Oppressive heat;
My mind in a whirl
I listen to the peals of thunder.
—Shiki

Ten

BY THAG POSSESSED

The weather in California is your friend. "Hey, dude," it says, "you wanna hang out in T-shirts and shorts all year? No problem!" The weather in England is a peevish and unpredictable antagonist that was sent to boarding school in its youth, got unmercifully bullied, and has been taking it out on the populace ever since. It doesn't talk to you. It prefers to communicate by means of rain, which it "sendeth on the just and on the unjust" exactly as stipulated in the Gospel of St. Matthew.

The weather in Japan is like her people. It obeys the rules, which are as follows:

Autumn	Winter	Spring	Summer
mild and sunny	dry and cold	mild and sunny	totally disgusting

Paul and Tessa had dropped a few hints about mildewed shoes and heat rash, but they failed to prepare me for the experience of summer in Tokyo. Indeed there's no way they could have prepared me, short of locking me in a jacuzzi for three months.

In June, spring packed her bags and fled, and summer shambled into Tokyo like some huge shaggy troll, all hot breath, sweaty paws, and body odor. The temperature soared into the nineties. The humidity approached one hundred percent. The sun vanished behind a horizontal curtain of gray haze. It was so dark outside that from my cubicle windows, closed for the summer due to air conditioning, I could barely see the trees across the street. It looked like a cold bleak winter in the northeast of England, the landscape obscured by the North Sea fog that the locals call "fret." I'd sit in the office thinking "winter in Yorkshire," and then I'd walk outside into a steam bath.

A *dark* steam bath. Japan does not use the system that we call "daylight savings" and the English, with their greater gift for poetry, call "summer time." The sun is on the side of Japanese bosses, who fear that if it stays light in summer till, say, eight o'clock, people might want to leave work early to play softball or something. There's no such thing as a long summer evening in Tokyo. By seven o'clock the sky is black as squid's ink. Not that it matters, because once the troll's around you live in perpetual twilight anyway.

I turned on my apartment's air conditioner, a unit stuck on the bedroom wall, and left it on until October.* It kept my apartment reasonably cool and dry, but the troll lurked just outside my metal door, ready to pounce. I called him Thag. "Down, Thag!" I would say as I pedaled to work. Thag ignored me. By the time I got to the office I was soaked with sweat.

"As your Japanese correspondent," I wrote home, "I've been an underachiever. I'm delinquent because I'm deliquescent, and that's the only humor to be had from humidity. For the past three days the depressing view from my office window—of the hideous apartment block next door—has been made even more

* It is probably unnecessary to add that HPJ paid my utility bills.

depressing by water oozing like colorless blood from a wounded sky."

Given the presence of Thag, rain was definitely redundant. But rain is Thag's best friend. The end of May brings what Baedeker's calls the *summer rainy season*, marked by sultriness, no wind, overcast skies, high humidity, and a "fine and penetrating" rain. "Leather, paper, etc., tend to be affected by mildew." The Colemans hadn't been kidding about their shoes.

Late July and August, Baedeker's goes on to confide, can be oppressively hot. Summer ends in mid-September with the *typhoon rainy season*, which can be distinguished from the *summer rainy season* by the fact that the rain falls horizontally as well as vertically.*

One Friday evening I emerged from the HPJ office into a downpour. I had ridden my bike to work, but a girl gets sentimental about her first typhoon. I thought the event called for special treatment, so I went back inside and asked the security guard to phone for a taxi. While I stood inside the front door waiting, several young people, not SPN members, arrived for an evening class. One of the boys decided to try out his idioms on me.

"I am soaked clear through to my skin!" he said proudly.

"*Ah sō desu ka.*"

He beamed at me. "It is raining dogs and cats!"

The twist made the cliché register. Through the glass door, I saw a shower of bewildered collies and cross-eyed Siamese cats falling onto the Inokashira Dōri.

"You speak good English," I said.

"Ah, sank you very much."

Next morning, the rain had stopped, but leaves were shivering on the cherry trees down the lane. I opened the two sets of sliding glass doors in my living room, leaving the screen doors shut, to catch the breeze, although it felt less like a breeze than

---

* "Typhoon" is Chinese for "big wind."

like Thag breathing heavily. In other words, it was a warm breeze, but it was better than nothing as I sat there drinking coffee and listening to Bob Dylan. Bob was on the first chorus of "Idiot Wind" when Thag took the hint and blew out one of the screen doors. Luckily it got stuck against the balcony and I was able to retrieve it before it flew down the street and beheaded one of my neighbors.

I learned a lot that summer. I learned that it's possible to ride a bicycle in a typhoon while holding an umbrella; that it takes about half an hour for sweat-soaked clothes to dry in an air-conditioned office; that "anti-perspirant" works only up to a point; and that when an air-conditioning unit leaks on a tatami mat, the results are not happy from the tatami mat's point of view.

I also learned about cicadas. This took a while because so much of my life is lived in my head that I'm not always as observant as I should be. If I'm working out the plot for Chapter 6, say, or engaged in a sexual fantasy, I can sit oblivious on a broken-down Number 2 Clement bus in San Francisco for half an hour after everyone else, including the driver, has got off.

So when I began to hear a hissing noise every time I went outside, I put it down to an overload of electricity in the wires and tried to think no more about it. But the hissing kept getting louder. The air was full of insistent sibilance, as if Tokyo were a giant tea-kettle perpetually on the boil.

"Miyuki-*san*," I said one day at the office, "I keep hearing this hissing noise."

"Hissing, Rhiannon-*san*?"

"Like this: SSSSSS . . ."

"Oh yes. It is the cicadas."

"Cicadas?"

"They are a kind of cricket."

"You mean *bugs*?"

"Yes, they are a kind of bug, I suppose."*

"But what are they doing?"

"I don't know," said Miyuki, casting her eyes down in a maidenly fashion which suggested to me that she did know, and that those crickets were not just having fantasies, they were, like, *doing it,* rubbing their legs together, finishing off with one partner and hopping up to the next, wings spread, mouths—do crickets have mouths?—wide open with satisfaction and delight. . . .

"Oh! Well, thank you, Miyuki-*san*."

"You're welcome."

The top of Paul's head appeared over his partition, followed by his eyes, his nose, and finally his beard. "Has Miyuki-*san* told you, Nano?"

"Told me what?"

"She's not a secretary any more."

"She has *been* promoted," Yoz piped up.

It was Paul's idea, bless his pointed beard. Most of the other women at HPJ were secretaries. There were one or two female engineers, but Miyuki wasn't qualified as an engineer, so Paul created a new job title for her: "marketing assistant." Even this modest advance was objected to by higher management, on the grounds that promoting one woman above the others might lead to unhappiness, Miyuki would be quitting soon to get married, the young men wouldn't like it, etc. Actually the young men didn't seem to mind at all, and Ikeda, Miyuki's boss, was all in favor.

Having done one brave new thing, HPJ decided to do another, and hired a married woman (gasp!) to replace Miyuki as secretary. Christine Yamada, a pretty young woman with round glasses and short wavy hair, had worked for HPJ before. As a

* Cicadas belong to the insect family Cicadidae, having broad heads and membranous wings. It's the males who make all the noise, using what my dictionary calls "a pair of resonating organs."

recent graduate with a degree in chemistry from a top university, she had applied for a job as engineer. She was amply qualified, HPJ admitted, but she was a woman. How would she like to be an executive secretary? So Christine had served as secretary to HPJ's president until she left to have her first child, a son. Now, with Yosuke in school, she agreed to come back and serve as secretary for the SPN group.

Christine recounted this story without detectable anger or regret in a voice that sounded as American as mine. Her mother was Japanese-American and Christine had gone to American schools in Switzerland, where her father had worked for the Japanese consulate. Christine was not only qualified to be an engineer, she was also fully bilingual in two of the world's most difficult languages.

I didn't want to believe that anyone could speak perfect, like-a-native English and also perfect, like-a-native Japanese. In other words, I didn't want to believe that anyone could be that much smarter than I am (despite ample evidence to the contrary).

So one day I asked Yoz if Christine spoke good Japanese.

"*Not* good," Yoz replied, in his emphatic way, and my spirits rose. He smiled. "*Excellent.*"

Despite her new title, Miyuki's duties did not appear to change, and for a while it seemed that nothing had been accomplished except that we now had two bilingual university graduates serving our morning and afternoon tea. But one day, soon after Christine joined us, the two of them issued a memo. It was written (Yoz told me) in hyper-polite Japanese, and stated that, "due to the pressure of much work," Miyuki and Christine were regretfully discontinuing the service of morning tea.

Weeks passed. The men of SPN did not grow weak with thirst or faint from lack of caffeine. It was discovered that all of them knew how to pour boiling water over tea leaves. They were able to keep working, and Ebisu moved ahead on schedule.

As a feminist, I kept waiting to get roiled-up about the oppression of Japanese women. But, in the first place, nobody ever tried to oppress *me*. If I'd gone to Japan in 1985 under other circumstances, not as a Foreign Service Employee for a Japanese-American company, I might have encountered the kind of sexism that I'd read about at home. But the Tomodachi were always respectful. In the second place, the women I saw in Tokyo didn't look oppressed; or maybe what I mean is that the men seemed even more oppressed than the women. While their husbands worked ten- to fourteen-hour days, the women were free to jaunt around Tokyo on trains, take classes, go to shows, do their bits of shopping. Undoubtedly they worked hard at home, but they had more autonomy and, once their children were in school, more leisure time than the men.

I learned too that most Japanese men turned over their paychecks to their wives, retaining an "allowance" for bar-hopping and golf. The wives handled the family finances, chose the vacation spots, and made most of the decisions about the children's education. On the home front, they wielded considerably more power than most of the Englishwomen I had met in the 1970s. In those days, my ex-husband was considered liberal because he "permitted" me to share his checking account.

So I wasn't troubled about the oppression of women. Not at first, that is. Still, I thought it was a shame that Miyuki and Christine had to keep serving tea in the afternoon.

Eventually Miyuki and Christine issued a second memo, couched in outrageously polite Japanese, canceling the service of afternoon tea.

I began to wonder if I'd misjudged my Japanese colleagues. They seemed so docile, so willing to toe the company line, so disinclined to say "boo" to a goose—yet while I was puttering around with light switches and window latches, Miyuki and Christine had quietly staged a revolution. A small one, but symbolic. It was a start.

And the two women were ahead of their time. In 1999, new guidelines went into effect for the treatment of women employees in Japanese Government offices. One of the guidelines: women can no longer be required to serve tea.

Eleven

✖

HERE COMES THE SCOOP SUMMER!

In July I spent a week in California. My Aunt Catherine, my father's sister, had written to say that she and Uncle Hal would be glad to see me sooner than Christmas, when I'd planned to take my first vacation. This was her way of letting me know that Hal, aged seventy-five, who'd been fighting prostate cancer, would probably not survive until the holidays.

A friend picked me up at San Francisco Airport and took me to his Cow Hollow apartment to sleep off my jet lag. As we drove into the city, I kept swiveling my head around, looking up and down Franklin Street. "What's the big event?" I asked.

"Come again?"

"Something must be happening today. There's hardly anyone on the sidewalks."

"Rhiannon, this is normal for San Francisco."

"Oh." I had forgotten what "normal" looked like.

I spent the rest of my visit in San Jose at my aunt and uncle's house. For once, my family's system of ignoring anything that "isn't nice"—an elastic term that covers everything from bad breath to near-suicidal depression—came in handy. It was easy to persuade myself that my uncle—a retired engineer and ac-

complished fisherman who looked like a compact edition of
Ernest Hemingway—was lying on the sofa, thin-faced and pale,
simply because he was overtired. An illegitimate son of Russian immigrants who grew up in a New York City orphanage,
Hal was a Republican, a self-made "man's man," and during
my counter-culture days we'd had screaming arguments. *I* had
screamed, anyway. Especially when he told me that if I hated
the U.S. so much, I should go live in the Soviet Union.
AMERICA: LOVE IT OR LEAVE IT was my uncle's motto. I
had left America, several times, but it did not escape his notice
that I kept coming back.

The TV was always on when Uncle Hal was at home, always tuned to some male fairy tale, a Western or a cop show, in
which few words were spoken and every argument was settled
with fisticuffs or gunplay. My uncle loved those programs—
"Maverick," "Bonanza," "The A-Team"—except when women
intervened in the form of "love interest," which didn't interest
him at all. "Mush," he always said, when a couple kissed. As
we women talked in the kitchen and my father (bookish, intro-
verted) sat at the dining room table trying to work a crossword
puzzle, shots rang out from the family room. The good guys
had won again, but not *because* they were good, only because
they shot straighter or had more reliable weapons. Slip those
cattle thieves a couple of thermo-nuclear devices and there'd
be no more family parties down on the Ponderosa, Hoss.

The TV was off for this visit. Uncle Hal was more interested in talking and even listening. He must have been in con-
siderable pain, but he didn't show it. He was dying sooner than
he wanted to, but he didn't show that either. My aunt, who as a
young woman had nursed her father, her mother, and her sister
through their last illnesses, was serenely competent as always
and gave no sign that she was performing the same service for
her beloved husband. I was encouraged to babble on about my
experiences, as though sitting bored and homesick in a Tokyo

office building and confronting tentacles at the supermarket were life's toughest challenges.

One afternoon I dropped in at the SPN office, where my colleagues had a bone to pick with me about the external specifications for Ebisu. "Who wrote this," they demanded, waving the copy I had sent them, "some Japanese guy who doesn't speak much English?" Rather than give them an honest answer— "Yes"—I volunteered to rewrite the specifications. Specs aren't usually a writer's responsibility, but I was tired of working on my haiku:

When your skirt hits the sky
And your clothes don't stay dry
That's a typhoon

Go for it, crickets!
She said, moments before
Her sandal squashed them flat

Working on the specs back in Tokyo, I learned more than I wanted to know about aisles, stockers, FIFO, and JIT (manufacturing terms: "First In, First Out" and "Just In Time"). I would struggle with a concept, filling pages with notes and diagrams. Then I'd trundle along to Duncan and show him the results, and he would look them over and say, "Not bad, Rhiannon, but you've left out the node-machine relationship, and you keep forgetting that a station can perform more than one operation." He'd cover my diagrams with ugly red ink and I'd slouch back to my desk and start all over again.

At least there was less cigarette smoke to breathe, because the Colemans had taken Yoz to California on a business trip. "Yoz is already contributing to marketing and not just learning," Paul wrote. "He was a good choice for this job." Yoz wrote to assure me that he wasn't too homesick. "Last weekend I went to Healdsburg, the hometown of Paul and Tessa. At night, it was so fine and so fine. We found so many shooting stars in the dark sky full of stars."

Taking advantage of Paul and Tessa's absence, I had the Marshalls over for dinner, together with Spats and Miyuki. Entertaining the Marshalls was tricky because Tessa always wanted to know what I'd done over the weekend. If I told her I'd seen Duncan and Linette, she'd get mad at me. If I lied—well, Tessa always seemed to know when I lied. Or at least she was good at giving that impression.

"This is the summer of my discontent," I wrote home, "here in the land of the perpetually damp armpit, where water fills the air and falls out of it at the same time. 'Sometimes too hot the eye of heaven shines, and often is his gold complexion dimmed' (Shakespeare), but usually not simultaneously, except in Tokyo in August. I am making no progress with either Ebisu or Japanese. I think my brain has mildewed."

The country continued to mystify me. What, for example, did the Japanese mean by covering products with senseless English slogans? Tessa and I began a collection of these, not necessarily buying the products, just writing down the words.

From the front of a sweatshirt:

> TIME FOR VISIT MESSAGE:
> LET BE

From the back of a jacket:

> Attention!
> Don't touch me with careless
> Cause I'm a nervous bomb

On a T-shirt: HALF GIRL, raising the immediate and pressing question, "Which half?" On a box of face cream that came free with a dress from the "Scoop" product line: "Look, Here comes the Scoop Summer! You can get varieties of Scoop terrific items. It's time now you have to distinguish yourself. You've got an opportunity to better looks on bright outfits by Scoop."

I found a brand of toilet paper called "My Fannie," funny enough in the U.S. but downright hilarious in Britain, where "fanny" is slang for "vagina."* Bags of Dutour brand coffee, available in many offices, made this irresistible offer: EASE YOUR BOSOMS. And I still cherish a set of paper napkins that are decorated with flowers and the following legend:

> FRESH AIR, FRESH EARTH
> BLOW IN THE WIND OF PLENTIFUL CALIFORNIA
> ALL PEOPLE IS LIVING IN HAPPINESS
> © Mellow Land Planning Company Inc.

But my favorite slogan was one that Tessa found on a doll's T-shirt. "Milk," it said. "I want to be in a cup." The more I looked at those words, the more convinced I became that they possessed some mystic significance. They were a Zen koan, I thought, like the sound of one hand clapping, and if I studied them long enough I would attain enlightenment.

I had ample time to study them because Tessa had put the T-shirt on "Burt," a plastic toy about six inches tall, olive drab in color and repellent in appearance, representing an Australian frilled lizard. Miyuki told us that in 1984 there had been a frilled-lizard craze in Japan, a country much given to crazes, because of an animated character on a children's TV program. Frilled lizards, she explained, are native to Australia. Tessa had found Burt lying in one of Tokyo's nameless streets when she first came to Japan. Something about him appealed to her—it was hard to see what exactly—so she dusted him off and brought him to work. He stood on her desk and, as the months passed, endured a succession of metamorphoses.

---

* When traveling in Britain, try not to refer to the wallet strapped around your waist as a "fanny pack."

In April, dressed in a paper robe and armed with a toy sword, he was Burt-*san*, *samurai* warrior. In June, when the "We Are the World" craze struck Japan and every electronics store in Kichijoji broadcast the recording session, repeatedly, on huge TV screens in the streets, the *samurai* warrior was transformed, via headband and cardboard guitar, into rock 'n' roll hero Bruce Springburt. In July he was the Statue of Liburty; in December, Saint Nicholburt.

The Tomodachi found Burt amusing, although it's possible that what they really found amusing was the spectacle of two grown women making costumes for a plastic lizard. But Ito-*san* came to our cubicle once, and there was a glint in his eye when he looked at Burt that made me wonder if we weren't transgressing another company rule. (Employees shall not keep plastic frilled lizards in their cubicles.)

I envied Burt his ability to change identities. I wished I could change mine. If only I were taller . . . thinner . . . smarter . . . richer . . . owned a closet full of Ellen Tracy separates and had a posh English accent, then surely interesting attractive men would follow me all the days of my life, and I would dwell near the House of Lords forever. (Kensington would do, or Barnes or Hampstead.)

Resting between identities, Burt wore his "Milk, I want to be in a cup" T-shirt, and I continued to ponder those words as if deciphering them would bring about the transformation I longed for. While waiting to get thin, smart, rich, well-dressed and English—there was no hope of getting taller—I made costumes for Burt. He changed on an almost weekly basis, but I went right on being the same.

Twelve

✦

THE LOST UMBRELLA OF IZU

I was invited to dinner *chez* Yamaguchi. This was an honor: the Japanese, mindful of their small houses, don't often entertain at home. (Their yards, they say, are "the size of a cat's forehead.") But Yamaguchi-*sensei* had rather a large house in East Takaido, shared with her husband, a chemistry professor at Keio University.

I arrived bearing flowers (not white chrysanthemums). I wasn't the only guest. Mrs. Yamaguchi (as I shall henceforth call her so I don't have to keep typing "*sensei*") must have been anxious about my unmarried state, because she had attempted a bit of sly matchmaking. My fellow guest was another pupil of hers, an English employee working in the Tokyo office of a multinational firm. His first name was something English like "Simon" or "Colin." Or possibly "Nigel." Mrs. Yamaguchi beamed upon us as she performed the introductions, but my heart sank. I was at least ten years older than Nigel. I was also American. It was hard to tell which he considered the more grievous offense. He wasn't my cup of tea either, but it seemed like good manners to conceal our differences, a fact that he might have been too young to appreciate.

"Rhiannon-*san* writes documentation for semiconductor software," said Mr. Yamaguchi, whose English was excellent and who seemed to be in on the plot. He encouraged Nigel, a semiconductor engineer, to tell me about his work. An American semiconductor engineer would have told me about his work, but Nigel, with the benefit of his Oxford education, knew that a mere woman wouldn't be able to grasp the subtleties of his chosen profession.

"I'm afraid it's *rah*-thuh complicated," he said, with a patronizing smile.

"Are you working with gallium arsenide?" I asked.

For the rest of the evening he ignored me. If he had opted to question me further, he'd have discovered that "gallium arsenide" was a bow drawn almost entirely at a venture. In fact I am *not* able to grasp the subtleties of his chosen profession, and would have admitted so readily, given the chance.

We sat down to dinner. I ate a lot of white rice. Mr. Yamaguchi ate a bowl of *natto*, a soybean paste that smells like all the mildewed shoes in Nishi Eifuku. The unfortunate Nigel, his sensibilities assaulted on all fronts, grew more and more reserved. I filled the resulting vacuum with bright superficial chat. As the evening wore on, we moved steadily away from each other in the direction of our national stereotypes. The more Nigel retreated, the more I, like a third-world nation, emerged. His upper lip stiffened, while mine quivered with readiness to tell all. The Yamaguchis looked on in amazement.

Back at the office, plans were being made for an SPN retreat to the Izu Peninsula. I had never heard of the place and the name "Izu" did not inspire confidence. It sounded like a sneeze. But Baedeker's promised "varied and beautiful scenery," "hot springs" (*Izu* means "spring"), and "romantically situated spas," so I agreed to go, even though it meant getting up early on a holiday.

We car-pooled in seven vehicles, an interesting experience that pointed up the Japanese fondness for doing things in groups.

All seven cars had to leave Tokyo at the same time and from the same place. We met at the McDonald's in Takaido. On the way to Izu, we stopped at a freeway service area to refresh ourselves. My car, driven by the solid and reliable George, arrived first. The last car, driven by the dashing young Easy Rider, who perhaps found it harder to maneuver than his motorcycle, arrived some forty minutes later. The rest of us were still there, long since refreshed but unable to depart because *we weren't all together*. Never mind that as soon as we hit the freeway we'd be separated again. Never mind that we'd be meeting just a few hours hence at our "pension" in Izu. We waited, the Japanese contentedly, we Americans in a fever of impatience to be getting on with the program.

The pension was a white wood-paneled building, set on a hill thick with trees. From the flat roof we could see over the treetops to the Pacific Ocean. There were two activities on offer: playing tennis or going to the beach. I have never been able to work up any enthusiasm for putting balls through hoops, over nets, into holes, etc. I mean, it's fine with me if the ball just lies there. My method of playing tennis, in the days when I had to because the gym teachers were bigger than I was, was to stand still, hold out my racquet, and hope that the ball would hit it. The C's I got in PE dragged down my grade point average, but even then I didn't care.

So I went to the beach. In a competition with the beaches of California, our beach in Izu would have rated no higher than Miss Congeniality. The sand was gray and the waves were flat-chested. They came in and went out with a wincing, don't-let-me-bother-you shrug that made me long for the assertive feminist surf at Santa Cruz. The color was off, too, an anemic washed-out blue. But, hey, I was outdoors and I wasn't sweating. After four months in Thag's embrace, that alone was worth the price of admission.

The price of admission was a shameful display of female anatomy. My bathing suit, borrowed from Tessa, was a lavender cotton one-piece that lacked any sort of interior bra arrangement. I'm not lavishly endowed by American standards, but by Japanese standards I was built to the max, and the Japanese are so averse to visible nipples that you can buy, in ordinary grocery stores like Summit, sticky circles of plastic to paste over the potentially offending appendages.

Foreseeing the difficulty, I had plonked down my hard-earned yen for a package of these devices. In my room in the pension, I opened up the package and took out a nipple-cover. Culture shock. It was the size of a nickel, whereas my requirement—a hasty glance down to assess the coinage—was for something the size of a silver dollar.

There was nothing to do but sit on the beach in a hunched position with my arms folded over my chest. The Japanese are camera-mad, so I have plenty of photographs that show me doing this. They are only slightly less embarrassing than the photographs that show me forgetting to do this.

I also have photographs of my colleagues frolicking in the surf and of Miyuki and another secretary (Christine hadn't joined us yet) sitting together, neither one displaying anything unseemly. I have photographs of Easy Rider blowing up an inflatable football. I have photographs of Stars and George taking photographs.

The entire retreat was recorded by camera. SPN manager Okada feeding his baby boy with chopsticks. Mr. Goodwrench, released from bondage to the SPN computer, raising a glass of wine to his pretty young wife. Ito-*san* smiling, or at any rate not frowning. Spats, sun-tanned and gorgeous in immaculate white shorts and knee-socks, holding a tennis racquet and grinning. Amiable Teddy flashing a peace sign. Yoz wearing a T-shirt lettered, "Cocaine is God's way of telling you you're making too much money." Miyuki looking beautiful.

My favorite photograph shows me with Ikeda's six-year-old daughter, Ayako. We're down at the beach at night. Aya-

chan,* in a pink skirt and gray vest with kitties on it, is standing
on a rock and leaning against me. I'm standing behind the rock
with my arms around her. I look happy, which I was, and not
like a woman who has chosen not to have children because she
wants to write books instead and is usually okay with that decision, but not when she's with a child like Aya *chan*. Which I
also was. In the background the lads are setting off *hanabi* (fire-
works), for no good reason ("It's a tradition," they explained to
Tessa solemnly). The air around Aya-*chan* and me is filled with
strings of golden light.

Tessa and I spent our last afternoon in Izu together. We
walked through green and gold woods down to a rocky cove
between gray cliffs, where I sat for a while and watched the
water. Uncle Hal used to fish in the Pacific, on boats out of San
Francisco or Half Moon Bay. My aunt would get up when he
did on the days when he went fishing, at three or four o'clock in
the morning, and make him sandwiches and a thermos of coffee. He'd kiss her ("Mush") and head out, wearing the flannel
shirt she'd made for him, "Hal's fishing shirt." In the evening
he'd come home tired and happy, sometimes empty-handed,
sometimes with half a dozen salmon, which he shared with the
neighbors.

Hal had died on September 6, at home, with Aunt Catherine
holding his hand. A week later, some of his friends took a boat
out of Half Moon Bay and scattered his ashes in the same ocean
that was splashing on the rocks around me. He and Aunt
Catherine had known in July that he was dying. I had known it
too, but they had helped me pretend I didn't. She had hidden
her grief, he had joked through the pain, so my last few days
with him could be happy ones, so I could say, "See you in December!" and fly back to Japan, so I could go on with my life.

For years I had wanted to say to my uncle, about those TV
programs he loved so much, that on the subject of courage they

---

* *Chan* is an honorific attached to shortened forms of children's names.

are one-dimensional. There are so many other ways to be brave, I wanted to tell him. Protesting against a war you believe to be unjust is brave, I wanted to tell him.

As it turned out, he knew all about being brave.

I leaned over and ran my hand through the water. It was cold.

Tessa followed me as I walked out of the cove and down a trail. "We'd better head back," she said.

"I *am* headed back."

"But the penchant is north."

"Pension. And this *is* north."

"South."

"Tessa, you direction-impaired peasant, the Pacific is on our left. Ergo, we're going north."

"But we're in Japan, Nano. Remember?"

I tried to visualize it. (Spatial reasoning is not one of my strong points.) "My God," I said. "You're right. I'm sorry, I forgot. We're upside down."

"Upside down in Izu," sang Tessa.

"It really doesn't please you—"

"And I don't mean to tease you—"

"But a strange feeling will seize you—"

"When you're upside down in Izu!"

Heading north on a different trail, we came upon an old black umbrella lying open and abandoned on its back in a field of rocks and lime-green sea-grass.

"Look!" I said, gesturing dramatically.

"What?"

"Over there! Don't you know what that is? It's the Lost Umbrella of Izu!"

"Oh wow," said Tessa, playing along. "And I've been thinking it was mystical."

"Mythical."

"We're lucky we got to see it."

I made her wait while I took a photograph. She didn't understand why I wanted to record the umbrella's existence and neither did I, until I got the photo back from the developer. The umbrella looks so vulnerable lying there, open to the sun and the rain, all by itself and miles from any of its fellows, in a country where no one wants to be alone.

AUTUMN

The mountain grows darker
Taking the scarlet
From the autumn leaves.
—Buson

Thirteen

AT THE SIGN OF THE STUFFED RACCOON

One day toward the end of September, Thag roused himself, looked around, decided he'd made a sufficient number of people miserable for long enough, and splodged away to hibernate for nine months. Or, to put it another way, cooler air masses swept in from mainland Asia and drove the hot air masses south. I switched off my air conditioner and the HPJ financial department breathed a collective sigh of relief. They were not, after all, going to have to sell the company to pay my electric bill.

Timing her visit neatly to coincide with Thag's departure, a friend from SPN product marketing came to Tokyo from California. Her object was to learn about the Ebisu software. Jeri Ann Smith belonged to the post-flower-power generation that spent its twenties getting MBAs from prestigious universities instead of backpacking around Europe in bell-bottomed trousers. Her MBA was from Stanford and she could use phrases like "position ourselves to penetrate the market" without blushing. She was unlike me in other ways too. She spent all her free time either bicycling up mountains or skiing down them, depending on the season. If she'd been in the Century Hyatt Hotel during an earthquake, she would have thrown on her sweats and made it down all twenty-two flights of stairs before the shaking stopped.

Her visit coincided with a national holiday for the autumn equinox, and Ikeda offered to take us on an overnight trip. We left Tokyo on a wet gray morning: Jeri Ann and me, Miyuki and Yoz, Ikeda and his daughter, Aya-*chan*, who moved into my lap for the weekend and into my heart forever.

Our first destination was Japan's most sacred mountain. This was my second attempt to see Fuji-*san*. On my first attempt, the fabled mountain had stayed hidden in mist. But that had been in May and this was September, which was, Ikeda assured me, a much better time of year for Fuji-viewing.

While we waited for the snow-capped summit to appear, I told Jeri Ann that Mount Fuji is a strato-volcano about three hundred thousand years old, twenty-five miles in diameter and 12,389 feet high. In early times it was revered as the home of the gods. When Buddhism was introduced to Japan, Fuji-*san* came to be seen as the gateway to another world. Until 1868, women were banned from Fuji-*san*, as well as from Japan's other natural shrines. Just when you think you've heard it all, patriarchy-wise, along comes a men-only mountain.

Jeri Ann was impressed by these facts, which I had memorized the day before from my Baedeker's. Aya-*chan*, no doubt thanking her lucky stars that she hadn't learned English yet, sat in my lap with my arms around her and gazed out the window at the view, which did not include Fuji-*san*. What we did see, as Ikeda's posh Toyota purred up the steep slopes, was a truly tremendous amount of fog. I'd spent four years in San Francisco and five years in England, but I'd never seen anything like it.

There are five routes up the mountain, each divided into ten stages. At the fourth stage on our route, 4000 feet up, Ikeda parked and we got out of the car. The fog had turned into rain, so we paused to attire ourselves in raincoats and umbrellas. Then we clambered up the mountainside to a point from which, Yoz assured us, there was a magnificent view on the two days a year when the fog disperses. He promised us that he personally had seen this view and that it includes five lakes. We took his word for it.

As the car purred back down the mountain, the feminine part of the party, the Back Seat, was so overcome by the grandeur of the scenery we hadn't seen that we fell asleep, leaving the masculine part of the party, the Front Seat, to get on with the driving. The Front Seat coped, and when the Back Seat regained consciousness we had arrived at our *ryokan* (Japanese inn).

As soon as I entered the lobby, I felt at home. During my earlier visit to the area, I had stayed in a *ryokan* that had a stuffed weasel in the lobby. I don't mean "stuffed" as in Teddy bears. I mean "stuffed" as in dead animals that have been interfered with by taxidermists. This new *ryokan* had a stuffed deer, a bee-hive, and a raccoon. The raccoon was standing up and wearing a little outfit (a round hat, a white scarf with blue polka dots, and straw sandals). Yoz explained (sort of) that the stuffed animals are supposed to make you feel that the establishment serves fresh and tasty food. That wasn't what they made me feel at all.

There are rules for staying in a *ryokan*. Inside the front door, you bow to the staff who have rushed out to bow to you. Then you remove your shoes. You can do this while making the acquaintance of the stuffed animals. You don't see your shoes again until you leave. Instead you wear unisex plastic slippers, except in the tatami-mat rooms, where you go barefoot, and in the bathrooms, where you change into toilet-specific slippers. All very hygienic, but the slippers will be too small for your big foreign feet and will cause you to trip on the stairs.

Dinner is served to your party in a private tatami-mat room. This gives you an opportunity to learn two things. The first is that Japanese legs are anatomically superior to your own. You and your Japanese friends sit on the floor around the low table with your calves folded under your thighs. After a few minutes, your calves send an urgent message to your brain—GIVE US BLOOD—so you unfold your legs and stick them under the table. After a few minutes, your back sends an urgent message to your brain—GIVE ME SUPPORT—so you twist your legs to the side. After a few minutes . . . Meanwhile, your Japanese friends are still sitting with their calves folded under their thighs. They can sit like that for hours.

The second thing you learn is just how much food there is in the world that you will not want to eat although your stomach is growling like an unstuffed raccoon. You don't get a menu, not that you could read it if you did. You don't get to ask if they have pizza. You get what they give you. I ate tempura, raw tuna, and wild-boar meat with alien vegetables, which left two-thirds of my dinner untouched, including the boiled snails and the whole baby trout. I explained my policy about not eating anything that has a head attached. "But the *head* is the best part," Yoz said, popping the trout's snout into his mouth.

Your room in a *ryokan* will be "traditional," by which the Japanese mean tatami mats on the floor, no furniture, and futons to sleep on. How the fluorescent light tubes and TV set fit into the tradition is not explained. The room I shared with Jeri Ann had one piece of decoration: a drawing of two tarantulas doing a mating-dance. I was afraid to ask Yoz what this was supposed to make me feel.

If by any chance it makes you feel like cuddling with your partner, you're out of luck unless you're gay, because the next item on the program is a long bath with members of your own sex. (In advanced *ryokans* both sexes bathe together, but nobody ever took me to one of those.) First you sit on a plastic stool to soap and rinse at a waist-high shower fixture. Only when you're clean do you enter the bath itself, which is kept hot with fresh water continuously bubbling up. Meanwhile the Japanese will keep an eye on you, partly because you look weird naked but mostly because they're afraid you'll commit an act that isn't forgiven even of foreigners: getting into the bath before you've bathed yourself.

After a soak, you climb into the cotton robe (*yukata*) provided by the *ryokan*. Everyone wears these blue-and-white robes for the rest of the evening, so as you stumble through the hallways in your plastic slippers, you have plenty of opportunities to feel like an idiot. Especially if you've belted the right side of your *yukata* over the left. Only dead people do this, apparently. Dead people and foreigners.

Jeri Ann and I were so relaxed after our bath that we fell asleep as soon as we hit the futons. I woke at about five a.m. when a rooster started crowing outside. "It's just a rooster," I thought, "what does it know?" So I went back to sleep until Yoz knocked on the rice-paper door. "*Excuse* me, ladies . . . now we would *like* to have breakfast."

In the main dining room, Jeri Ann, Yoz, Miyuki, Ikeda and Aya-*chan* sat on tatami mats in their *yukatas*, happily consuming seaweed pancakes, fish soup, fish, boiled white rice, and green tea. I sat on my calves (GIVE US BLOOD) and tried to ignore my stomach (GIVE ME COFFEE). Then we got dressed, collected our shoes, and said goodbye to the stuffed animals and the staff, who seemed sorry to see us go although I'd wasted so much of their food.

After another long drive, we reached the coastal town of Kamakura. But first, there were many hours of navigating through Japanese-holiday traffic for Ikeda, and many giggles for Aya-*chan* as Rhiannon practiced her Japanese. "*Kyō Kamakura ikimasu* (today we're going to Kamakura)" turned out to be hopelessly wrong. "*Kyō* wa *Kamakura* ni *ikimasu*," Aya-*chan* kindly corrected. I had forgotten my particles again.

Feeling defensive, I decided to teach Aya-*chan* how to count to ten in English. "One, two, three," I began, and gestured to indicate that she should repeat the numbers after me.

"Four, five, six," replied Aya-*chan*, "seven, eight, nine, ten . . ."

In Kamakura, Ikeda raised our cholesterol levels, which had dropped dangerously low, with a lunch of cheese fondue and milky coffee. Then Jeri Ann wanted to wade in the Pacific Ocean across the street. It was another wet gray day, but Japanese boys were trying to surf on the lowest-profile waves I had ever seen. Surf was definitely down. Aya-*chan* waded in after Jeri Ann, and I took pictures of the two of them standing in the flat pewter-colored water.

When we travel, we poke fun at flat surf and stuffed raccoons, boiled snails and invisible sacred mountains, by way of both admitting and denying that we're out of our depth and lonely and a long way from home. Japanese tourists in America write to their friends that the service is terrible and the rice tastes funny, and they're right. By their standards, it is and it does.

What I remember most about that weekend is my boss, Kenichi Ikeda, driving through bad weather and terrible traffic to share his country with us. He wanted to show us Mount Fuji, but instead he showed us himself, resilient, generous, and cheerful, and his daughter, who throughout two long days of travel never once cried or pouted or complained, but sat trustingly in the lap of a foreign stranger, singing songs to herself and tilting back her shining black head to smile at me.

Jeri Ann and I took the train from Kamakura back to Tokyo. My arms felt empty for days.

Fourteen

THE BEARS GO OVER THE MOUNTAIN

"It's three p.m.," I wrote to my friends the Thompsons, who live in London. "I know it's three p.m. because I'm writing from the office, and every day (*mainichi*) at this time, a recording is broadcast of someone plunking at the piano while, in the foreground, a harsh male voice tells us to exercise. '*Hai! Ichi, ni, san, yon* . . . (Okay! One, two, three, four . . .)' No one ever exercises. I find it rather sinister.

"I'm supposed to be documenting a Shop Floor Control system for semiconductor manufacturers. However, it seems likely that in a few weeks, my division of Hewlett-Packard will be 'obsoleted' and our product line 'matured.' HP will continue to support our existing customers, but will not make further changes to the software or sell it to new customers. I'm not supposed to know about this yet, but in my privileged position (good buddy to the boss's wife) I've been tipped off. The announcement won't be made for weeks. Meanwhile, I've been told to continue documenting code that may never be released in a manual that may never be published. Futility, thy name is software!"

When Tessa told me about the rumored obsolescence, my reaction was, "Thank God! Now I won't have to document reworks." I'd been harder hit by an earlier rumor that the SPN group would be moved from Takaido to the factory in Hachioji. Instead of a fifteen-minute bike ride to work, I'd be spending two and a half hours a day on strap-hanging trains. "Tessa and I are planning a sit-in protest," I wrote to colleagues at home. "We've already worked up a chant: 'Hachioji, we won't goji!'" I told Paul flatly that I'd return to California first, thus earning more black marks for Grace Under Pressure, or whatever the category was called on the Hewlett-Packard performance review.

That rumor was dispelled, but this one looked like it was coming true. Striving to sympathize with Paul and Tessa as they stared glumly into space or pounded out angry e-mail messages on their keyboards, I imagined that the experience was like having a novel rejected by every publisher in the English-speaking world. A bummer, but you could always write another novel.

The fate that hung over Paul and Tessa was the threatened closure of their tiny Hewlett-Packard office in Healdsburg, in the wine country north of San Francisco, followed by transfer to the dreaded Silicon Valley. At home, Paul could wheel and deal his way through anything—he had kept the Healdsburg office alive for years after HP started trying to kill it—but he wasn't at home. Could he pull off the trick from Japan? The hopes of the half-dozen other employees of the Healdsburg office, equally committed to *la belle vie* in Sonoma County, rested on him. It was a good thing he had broad shoulders.

My own reaction was to think, like the prince in the *Tale of Genji*, "I really was not made for this endless round of official business . . . I wonder if I shouldn't get away from it all and retire to a monastery." Badgered by rumors, irked by the feud between the Marshalls and the Colemans, and bored witless by months of insufficient work, I was so demoralized that shaving my head and turning Buddhist monk was starting to seem like a good idea.

I'd been in Japan for six months and I still hadn't started the Ebisu documentation. User manuals may not be the work I was born for, but if I must write them, I want them to end up in the hands of users. Oh, I'd been flippant about the Belgian semiconductor engineer, but I really did want to give him the Ebisu document. ("I wrote this for you, *Monsieur*. Please use it to improve your process flow.") Nor, in the circumstances, did my creative writing flourish. *Terminal Death* sat neglected in Nishi Eifuku while I spent eight hours a day helping Tessa write a user manual that would probably end up in the wastebasket. In the words of Gerard Manley Hopkins, I felt like "time's eunuch," unable to "breed one work that wakes."

I wasn't getting anywhere with the Tomodachi either. Mrs. Yamaguchi was still optimistic, but although I had a lot of *nihongo* in my head, it never seemed to translate into meaningful conversation. I could tell the lads, "I enjoy eating ice cream," or "I went to the department store yesterday," but where did that get us? Anything that I could say to them in Japanese, they could understand if I said it in English, and none of it was *omoshiroi* (interesting). Plain recitals of fact, stripped of affect and personality, are not the kind of communication that turns acquaintances into friends.

Not that it mattered. Fluent Japanese would have helped, but it wouldn't have made me good buddies with the Tomodachi. In my culture, friendship, at least for women, is built on shared confidences, confessions of doubt or failure, crows of delight, the occasional expression of joy, triumph, or sorrow. I'm not saying you have to be a fount of perpetually-spewing emotion, but if you keep everything bottled up, it's hard for people to feel close to you.

The Japanese are major bottlers. I didn't know why yet— something to do with *giri*-to-one's-name, probably—but I'd learned enough to grasp that even if I spoke *nihongo* like a native, the lads would not come dropping by my cubicle to dish.

George wouldn't tell me that he was jealous because Fingers typed faster than he did. Easy Rider wouldn't admit to late-night frolics with the *bōsōzoku* boys. Spats wouldn't bend my ear over a plate of *tempura* about problems with his girlfriend (if he had a girlfriend), and the Imp wouldn't confess that his mocking laugh hid the tears of a clown. Harpo wouldn't invite me to go bowling, or whatever it was he did for fun.

There was so much I didn't know about them! What had got Stars hooked on astronomy? Why was he willing to travel halfway around the world to take photographs of a comet? All his photos looked the same to me: tiny white dots in black space. What did they mean to Stars? Was the Imp as funny in Japanese as he seemed to be in English? Did he tell actual jokes—"Here's one about the traveling *sushi* salesman and the farmer's daughter"—or was he just witty in general? Did Mr. Goodwrench *like* being the systems guru, or had someone stuck him with the job? What did the other lads think of Paul—of Ikeda—of Ito-*san*—of me? Which lad was the best-liked? Who were the natural leaders? Who was the most articulate? Who was the smartest? Who knew the most *kanji*? Why didn't Harpo ever say anything? (He was capable of speech. I saw him murmur something to Spats once.)

By now, if they were American, I'd know where they were from, where they went to college, whether or not the single lads were dating anyone, who had kids, who was "management potential," who was lucky to have a job at all. I'd like most of them, because HP employees are usually likeable. Some would already be good friends.

Miyuki, Yoz, and Christine were friends, although there were things I would never learn about them because I couldn't imagine asking the relevant questions. But the other Tomodachi remained on their side of that impassable wall. Did they even like me? I couldn't tell from their body language. Even Japanese smiles can be deceptive—they don't necessarily mean "I like you" or "I'm glad to see you," although that's how I chose to interpret them.

I couldn't read the people any more than I could read their books. I was surrounded by colleagues for whom I felt already a kind of desperate, clutching affection, but whom I would never really get to know. I tried telling myself that the affection was related to the ignorance. Maybe if I knew the lads I wouldn't like them at all. Maybe they were foul-mouthed, spiteful, and depraved. Worse, maybe they were boring. But it didn't help much, mainly because I didn't believe it.

I wanted to go home, but that would have been letting the Tomodachi down. Even Ito-*san*, whom I suspected of deploring my refusal to be hammered down, was relying on me to deliver the goods. I didn't want to quit before I'd done at least one thing to repay HPJ for the cost of bringing me to Tokyo. Also, and equally important, I hadn't had time yet to save a suitcase stuffed with money.

It meant putting up with a lot. In the weeks after the rumor of obsolescence reached us, the office atmosphere, already thick with smoke and the bad vibes from Paul and Duncan's feud, thickened further with gloom. It was like living in one of those dark medieval paintings where you can't quite make out the people but they're probably Borgias, and you can tell that dragons are lying in wait just beyond the edge of the canvas.

But Thag was gone and autumn was with us, "season of mists and mellow fruitfulness, close bosom-friend of the maturing sun" (Keats). In Tokyo the mists were more in evidence than the mellow fruitfulness, but in the branches of a tree on Church Street, ripe orange-red persimmons hung like baby moons. Out in the country, Yoz told me, the phenomenon known as "flaming leaves" was underway.

I wanted to see the flaming leaves, but not by myself, so I inveigled my parents to Japan by the simple trick of paying for their airline tickets. Jet-lagged, culture-shocked, and dazed with the knowledge that their elder daughter had somehow acquired money to burn, they were putty in my hands. Mom was then seventy-one and Daddy was eighty-two, but off they went with me to Nikko, a town, says Baedeker's, renowned for its sumptuous tombs. Yes, for all your tomb-viewing holidays, Nikko's the place.

A popular Japanese catch-phrase is, "Never say 'magnificent' (*kekkō*) until you have seen Nikko." Guilty as charged. I had said "magnificent" lots of times, translated into Californian ("far out!"). Welsh waterfalls, Scots lochs, and the view from the Eiffel Tower had all elicited this superlative from me. I can't say that I was equally moved by the tombs of Nikko. I can't even say that I *saw* the tombs of Nikko. The hotel Tessa had recommended, the beautiful Nikko Prince, was on the shore of Lake Chuzenji, some miles out of town. From our windows there wasn't a tomb to be seen, but the flaming leaves were much in evidence. They lay scattered like fallen stars all over the green lawns that ran down to the lake, where the hills, corrugated with color, were mirrored in flat water. It looked as if the dye in the leaves had run down into the lake and stained it red, gold, and bronze.

"Package trips are for tourists," I told my parents. I should have known that it's pointless trying to play Sophisticated World Traveler for people who have seen you wearing diapers. I made all the arrangements for our trip myself, which was very enterprising and stupid of me. We would have seen more for a lot less money if I'd signed us up for the standard see-Nikko-and-its-sumptuous-tombs tour.

One morning we took the bus into Nikko to see the Toshogu Shrine. "Shrines are Shinto," I lectured my parents, as we walked toward our destination. "They have gates called *torii*, like a giant letter H with an extra bar across the top. The Japanese used to put live cocks on the *torii* as offerings to the Sun Goddess. The buildings are usually simple, except that they're often painted red-orange."

"Like the Golden Gate Bridge," said my father helpfully.

"Right. Now, temples are Buddhist—unpainted wood, not much decoration. It's the temples that have pagodas."

My mother nudged me and pointed. There at the entrance to the Toshogu Shrine stood a *torii* next to a pagoda. The Shogunate, which had the shrine built, had mixed images from both religions.

At the famous *Yomei-mon*, or Sunlight Gate, we paused long enough to pick up a brochure. "There are the tablet [*sic*] denoting the name of the temple, drawings of two dragons appearing on the ceiling of the porticos, *Mokume-no-toro* (wood-grain tiger) carved on one of the central columns, *Mayoke-no-sakasa-bashira* (Evil-averting Inverted Column), etc." We spotted the wood-grain tiger but not the evil-averting column, which made me wonder if foreigners weren't one of the evils that the column was inverted to avert.

Never mind. Beyond the gate lay twenty-two prime-shrine buildings. Starting in the seventeenth century, 15,000 workmen had come from all over Japan to work on the shrine. Every one of them had found something to carve, frill, or gild. Decoration had been laid on with a trowel, and then the decorations had been decorated. Even Baedeker's admits to an "over-lavish profusion." My mother, reared by people who considered crucifixes "in bad taste" and accustomed to Methodist churches with folding chairs instead of pews, was visibly nervous. I think she was afraid that a Buddhist priest might leap out from behind a portico and try to convert her.

On the premises is the mausoleum of the shogun Tokugawa Ieyasu, to whom, in 1617, the Emperor granted the title "Incarnation of the Bodhisattva Illuminating the East." Ieyasu was dead at the time, but no doubt grateful. A flight of two hundred stone steps leads to his resting-place. I looked at those steps, looked at my white-haired parents, and knew that I was destined never to see the spot whence the Incarnation continues to illuminate the East. Anyway, the steps were black with the heads of ascending and descending visitors. There was probably no room at the tomb.

The day before we left, I decided we should go on another outing, taking the bus away from rather than into Nikko. For this I blame my mother, who sang to me repeatedly in my childhood the song about the bear going over the mountain "to see what he could see." Certainly there was no other reason to head in that direction, although it was a jolly ride. We discovered that Japanese buses are equipped with spare metal seats that flap down into the aisle. The other seats being full, we perched on these as the bus raced around hairpin turns and the Japanese laughed delightedly at the looks on our faces.

We got out at another lake, where we walked around and took photographs of swans. Then we went and stood at the bus-stop to wait for a bus home. An hour passed. Shadows slanted across the lake. Mother swans circled, gathering up their cygnets. My mother pasted on her brave expression, the one that wouldn't fool a cat. I got mad because it was easier than admitting I'd done something stupid. Easier for me, that is.

I was trying to work up the nerve (and the vocabulary) to ask someone if he'd call a taxi for us—meanwhile objecting bitterly to the fact that Japanese phone books have the nerve to be printed in Japanese—when a young man pulled up in a shiny new car* and rolled down his window. "There will not be a bus for another hour," he said. "May I take you to your destination?" The Nikko Prince Hotel was on the young man's way, he assured us. But then he would have told us the same thing even if he'd been headed in the opposite direction.

My parents left Japan ten days later. They had missed most of the things I wanted to show them because, after the Nikko trip, we were too tired to do more traveling. Daddy never got to see Mount Fuji. Mom was not introduced to the Great Buddha

---

* Every car I saw in Japan was new and shiny. I don't know what they do with the old ones. Sell them to us, perhaps.

of Kamakura, in whose serene and ancient presence she might have felt something related to the peace that she finds in the Methodist Church. I had blown it. My parents were going home without having really seen Japan.

On our last evening together, I took them to Shinjuku for *shabu-shabu*, strips of meat and vegetables cooked in hot broth. Outside the restaurant, which was on the tenth floor of a high-rise building, I propped my handbag on a railing while I took my parents' picture. Half an hour later, I realized that I'd left the handbag behind. We found it sitting on the railing in that busy building with its contents intact.

"The people here are so honest!" said my father.

"And so kind," said my mother. "I'll never forget that young man who gave us the ride."

"And the people on the bus who showed us the folding seats."

"And your friends, Miyuki and Yoz, the way they came to the party you gave for us and brought us presents, even though they'd never met us before."

"And your boss, Mr. Ikeda, who said such nice things about you."

After all, I reflected, my parents had seen quite a lot of Japan.

Fifteen

FAST BOAT TO CHINA

I spent a bundle on my parents' trip. I made frequent visits to Tokyu *depāto*. I ate Shredded Wheat (fifty cents a biscuit) and Häagen-Dazs (four-fifty a pint). I served my dinner guests eight-dollar raspberries and, on one memorable occasion, a seventeen-dollar melon. (I had worked out the price as seven dollars, a reasonable amount to spend on a melon in Tokyo.) My new stereo had a CD player and I began to acquire a collection of compact disks. I took so many photographs that the owner of the store where I had them developed broke into smiles when he saw me coming.

And still the balance rose in the Fuji Bank account that Miyuki had opened for me. Since there seemed to be some danger that I might end up with serious money, as opposed to the frivolous, easily-spent kind I usually had, I took a week of unpaid leave in November and went to Hong Kong. My colleague Gail Lowell, who was a Foreign Service Employee at Samsung Hewlett-Packard in South Korea, flew in from Seoul the same day I flew in from Tokyo. Paul and Tessa were due to join us a day later.

137

Kai Tak airport was not like Narita. Every other car pulling away from the curb was a Rolls Royce. I settled for an ordinary taxi and enjoyed my chat with the driver. It had been a long time since I'd been able to hold a conversation in a cab. When we got to the Golden Mile Holiday Inn, he displayed an inclination to linger. I had to say, "Goodbye, have a nice day!" several times before he finally slid back into his taxi, looking sullen. I was in my room unpacking before I remembered that in Hong Kong, unlike in Tokyo, you're expected to tip.

Gail arrived a few hours later and we went out into the streets of Hong Kong to act like middle-class American women. In other words, we shopped. I specialized in shoes and trousers. Gail didn't specialize at all. I planned to branch out into blouses the next day, but Paul and Tessa insisted on seeing the sights. We cruised the harbor by boat and went up Victoria Peak on the funicular for the view of Hong Kong harbor at night. Next night we went again to see the lights running up skyscrapers, spangling the masts of ships, floating on the water, charging through streets, shining from every window.

We were all relieved to be in Hong Kong. The city felt looser, freer, than either Seoul or Tokyo: lots of nails sticking up. Here was a place where we didn't have to be on our best behavior, mindful at all times of our duty to present a Good Image of Americans Abroad. Plus the breakfast buffet at the Holiday Inn offered almost-forgotten delicacies like blueberry pancakes, maple syrup, and Canadian bacon.

We had an expensive, hilariously intoxicated Thanksgiving dinner at the top of the Hong Kong Hilton, Paul and Tessa's treat: four bottles of wine and all the Chinese food we could eat. We could eat plenty. I maintained decorum until the end of the meal, when a misunderstanding between my chopsticks and a bean shoot sent me into fits of giggles from which I only slowly recovered. Tessa and Gail told bawdy jokes—to be fair, they do this even when they're sober—and outside the restaurant, Paul found a statue of some long-dead dignitary that was begging to be climbed. We coaxed him down from the dignitary's bronze embrace, boarded the Star Ferry, and sailed back to Kowloon. The view of Victoria Peak from Hong Kong harbor at night is almost as spectacular as the other way round.

We did tourist things for several days and then the Colemans went back to Tokyo. Gail and I stayed on for one last adventure: a day trip into the People's Republic of China. We boarded a hydrofoil and an hour later got off on the island of Macau, which confusingly enough belonged to Portugal.* A Chinese person asked for my passport and returned it stamped "Corpo de Policia de Segurança Pública: S. Migração." Joyful at encountering a foreign language I could actually read, I wandered around reading things ("Eduardo Wong: Dentista") until a tour guide seized me and thrust me into a bus.

Macau and its two offshore islands occupy six square miles of territory, the guide informed us as we rattled up a street lined with banyan trees. The population was estimated at three hundred thousand. Their principal occupations, according to our guide, were gambling, prostitution, and drugs. He eyed Gail and me as if assessing the possibilities. We passed Number One Wife's house. Number One Wife was married to the actual governor of Macau, the casino owner. He lived near the ostensible governor, who came from Portugal. They got together every evening to talk about business.

We stopped at St. Paul's, a seventeenth-century Jesuit church, "the symbol of Macau." In 1835 it burned to the ground in a typhoon-fanned fire. Only the Baroque façade remains. Now there's a symbol that knows how to be symbolic. After taking its picture, there was not much to do but stroll around feeling like a well-heeled heel for fending off the souvenir-sellers. Or, of course, one could buy the souvenirs, a popular alternative for our fellow travelers, a jolly party of Australians.

---

* Officially, it's a Chinese territory under Portugese administration, returning to the People's Republic of China in December, 1999.

New bus, new tour guide. Ruth Loo introduced herself as "a citizen of the People's Republic of China." A Communist! Ruth was reading my mind. "We have a socialist government in China," she said firmly. Good heavens, then what has all the fuss been about?

We drove through a gateway. The people were suddenly very badly dressed. We weren't in China yet, but in a sort of barrier zone between East and West. We were led off the bus and into a Communist—sorry, *socialist*—building, where socialist officials examined our passports for signs of ideological rot. Finding nothing in mine but a tendency to hang out in the United Kingdom, they let me in.

We exited through a different door, and now we were truly in China. Walking about were a lot of people who made the barrier-zone folk look like snappy dressers. Most of them were carrying cabbages. The ones who weren't carrying cabbages were carrying ducks. The ducks were dead.

We were taken to a market, where we were allowed to wander around watching people sell fish. On the third floor of the market building was an area about the size of a broom cupboard: the clothes department. Chinese people sidled by, eyeing the bell-bottomed trousers with longing.

We got back in the bus and rode through country that looked like desert. I kept expecting to see camels, but what we saw instead were condominiums. That's what Ruth called them: condominiums. They were even uglier than buildings in Tokyo, a thing I would not have imagined possible. Ruth encouraged us to come and work in China so we could live in one of these condominiums. We hid horrified smiles behind our hands.

After lunch we started down a road so picturesque that I started praying for the bus to break down so I could get out with my camera. If you take pictures, you will know how a sudden juxtaposition of people and things, a flash of color, a tree-framed vista, screams, "Take me! Take me!" to the bearer of an erect camera. We passed about five hundred things like that.

Panting with photographer's lust, I stuck my camera out the window and shot a roll of film as we drove past duck farms, water buffalo standing in rice paddies, and oyster fishermen on the banks of the Pearl River. I took another roll of film at Sun Yat-Sen's boyhood home. His parents, with four eyes on the future eminence of their offspring, had obviously shopped around for the most picturesque place in southern China, and having found it, moved in.

The popularity of American culture makes it hard to find places that aren't full of the things you left home to get away from. Wherever you go, Hollywood movies, MTV, and Pizza Hut are there to greet you. Things may look a bit odd but they don't look completely foreign, not even in Japan, where the statues of Colonel Sanders are dressed in Santa Claus suits for Christmas and the department stores play "Silent Night" while you shop.

But China was foreign. It was a dream of traveling come true. Excited as I hadn't been in years, I bounced up and down in my seat and peppered poor Ruth with questions. "What about the Cultural Revolution?" I asked.

It had been, Ruth said, a bad thing. Many people had suffered. English books had been burned.

"Shakespeare?" I asked, anxious to get down to specifics.

"Oh, yes."

But now things were better. One of Ruth's teachers had been let out of prison. Women were allowed to wear skirts and make-up. Wages were rising. She, Ruth, earned about fifty dollars a month, plus two bags of rice. "How much do you earn?" she asked. Everyone on the bus went very quiet. I was earning almost that much an hour, but I of course had to buy my own rice.

Ruth's apartment was cheap. She shared it with five other women. She told us how the population has been kept stable by birth control.

"What happens," an Aussie wanted to know, "if you have a baby before you get married?"

"That cannot happen."

"But—"

"That is impossible," Ruth said firmly.

If all the single women are five to an apartment, you can see how it would be. But I was fascinated by the idea of a government doing battle with its people's collective libido. I was fascinated by Ruth. She had never been out of China. The people are not allowed to travel, but she hoped to go to Hong Kong in 1997. She had taught herself English with many American touches. "You want to take pictures? No problem."

I wanted to take pictures. I wanted to stay. I want to go back. I want to find Ruth and bring her home with me and show her San Francisco, the Sonoma coast, Yosemite, and Macy's. But her government won't let her go.

On the hydrofoil from Macau, I took out my passport and looked at the People's Republic of China stamp, a red circle with a star in it. I flipped through pages of arrivals and departures. Gatwick, Heathrow, Felixstowe, Narita. I held my passport all the way back to Hong Kong.

WINTER

New Year's Day:
The desk and bits of paper,—
Just as last year.
Matsuo

Sixteen

THE GOD OF GOOD FORTUNE

I fell in love with Hong Kong: the water, the hills, the boats, the ready supply of cheap Shredded Wheat. I could read street signs and newspapers. I could tell taxi drivers where I wanted to go instead of thrusting written directions at them, a convenience for which I was more than willing to tip. I could afford to buy clothes in Hong Kong. I could try on shoes that fit. (The largest women's shoe size in Tokyu *depāto* was six. I take eight and a half.) I could probably have found nipple-covers that fit, but I wouldn't need them in Hong Kong. I could turn on the TV and hear people speaking English. Not American English, either. Proper English. BBC English. Hong Kong was exotic and Asian but it was also reassuringly British. Yet I could sense China out there, just beyond my range of vision, like the dragons hovering outside the medieval painting: exotic, Asian, not British at all. Not American either.

In Tokyo, the city filled all the space that I could easily travel to or imagine. I couldn't sense anything beyond my range of vision: no ferries, no hills, no dragons. No mystery at all. I began to have waking nightmares that Tokyo was expanding to encompass the world, so that when I finally got free to leave it, there would be nowhere else to go.

By the time I got back, the flaming leaves had fallen. In Inokashira Park, the bare branches of the cherry trees traced patterns, fantastically articulated, against the dull gray sky. Siberian-chilled air scoured my face as I bicycled down Church Street to work, bundled up in an oversized wool jacket, boots, hat, and gloves.

I woke one morning much earlier than usual. It was oddly quiet outside and there was something different about the light in my bedroom. I wrapped myself in a robe and went out onto the living-room balcony. Snow had fallen in the night and lay folded like thick white blankets on the flat rooftops of Nishi Eifuku. On the small lawn across the street, where her father had practiced archery all summer, a little girl in a green sweater and a bright yellow cap was setting the head on a snowman. Two women went picking their way down the lane toward the Inokashira Dōri. They walked carefully, single file between the snow-plumped trees and bushes, carrying pink and yellow umbrellas.

Yuki wa honen no shirushi, says a Japanese proverb. "Snow is the sign of a fruitful year." But when I got to work that morning (on foot; I didn't want to chance my bike in a snowstorm), I found that the rumors had been confirmed. HP was "obsoleting" the SPN product line. Paul, Tessa, and Duncan were inconsolable. So were many of the Tomodachi. I felt bad for them, and worse because people kept using "obsolete" as a verb.

Paul and Tessa would be "repatriating" (going home) in April to an uncertain future. Worried e-mail messages were arriving hourly from their colleagues in the Healdsburg office, which HP would almost certainly close. "We love Healdsburg, Nano," Tessa said sadly.

I sympathized. When I'd joined HP in 1982, I was asked to document Paul's software. This had entailed frequent visits to the Healdsburg office. Driving the 120 miles north was like going backwards in time. Sonoma County was what the Santa Clara Valley had been before it turned Silicon, "the valley of heart's delight," all small towns, farms, and orchards. The Sonoma hills were apple-green in winter, straw-gold in summer. The valleys were planted with fruit trees and grapes. In sleepy small-town Healdsburg, Victorian frame houses surrounded a century-old, block-square Plaza, complete with bandstand. The Russian River wound around the town. Paul and Tessa had taken me wading there one night under a sky thick with stars.

"If I lived in Healdsburg I'd never want to leave," I told Tessa.

"We don't," she said, and turned back to her computer to read another e-mail message.

Guiltily, I wondered whether it was the cost of furnishing my apartment that had brought SPN, "the total solution for semiconductor manufacturers," to its untimely end. Or was Ebisu finally exacting his revenge? Maybe he didn't like having his name taken in vain any more than God did.

"If anyone's planning to visit," I wrote to friends in California and England, "I suggest you do so soon. At any moment HPJ will realize the folly of paying me to write documentation that no one will ever read. Stripped of my stripped-pine furniture, cast out on my street which must remain nameless since it doesn't have a name, I will end my days in Nishi Eifuku, cursing Ebisu, the god of good fortune, for turning his back on me."

For a while I worried that I'd be sent home early, without my suitcase stuffed with money. Then I realized that I couldn't go home early, because for tax purposes, I had declared myself a non-resident of California. If HPJ let me go, I would have to hole up somewhere until October. I could stay with English friends, but I'd have to give them something for my keep, and I wouldn't be able to earn any money. What would become of Bunter and my novel? Would HP pay to keep all my things in storage for an extra ten months?

Pondering these imponderables, struggling with Japanese, and trying to finish *Terminal Death*, I worked myself into what the English call "a right old state." My insomnia was worse than ever. Some nights I didn't sleep at all. I couldn't seem to make even simple decisions. Since arriving in Japan I had written fifteen chapters of my novel—130 pages. Now I was stuck.

It was too much. I couldn't work full-time, learn Japanese, cope with living alone in a foreign country, and write a sparkling, well-plotted mystery novel at the same time. I decided to set *Terminal Death* aside until I got back to California and focus instead on making the most of my time in Tokyo. This meant that I got to relax sometimes (read, listen to music, or just stare into space) without feeling guilty about it. My Japanese progressed because I actually took the time to study.

For a couple of weeks I felt much happier. Then, one evening when I wasn't looking, I sneaked into my study and read the completed chapters of *Terminal Death*. They weren't good enough either, so I threw them away and started on version three.

At work, I kept waiting for one of my bosses to call me into his cubicle and tell me that it was time to pack my bags. But which boss? I had three now, for Paul's replacement had arrived at the end of November to start learning his new job. Thirty-year-old Ken Matsuda, a second-generation Japanese-American from SPN in California, was also expected to "lend the SPN group his marketing expertise," i.e., help us sell more stuff. The products he was being asked to peddle were now "mature," but he was urged to look upon this as an added challenge.

Ken was a good-looking young man with a gift for wearing clothes as if both he and they had just been professionally laundered. With him around I felt more disheveled than ever in my rumpled skirts stained with bicycle grease, but I couldn't resent him; he was charm incarnate. I was also grateful for his presence as another diffuser of the tension between Duncan and the Colemans.

The snow melted gradually away from Tokyo. Bits of it lingered here and there, looking silly, like guests who've stayed too long at a party and will soon be asked to help clean up. All that remained of the short-lived snowman across the lane were the two yellow tennis balls that had constituted his eyes. In Kichijoji, where I did my Christmas shopping, the electronics shops were playing Beethoven's Ninth Symphony. ("It's a tradition," Yoz said.) It made a welcome change from "We Are the World," but even the Ode to Joy couldn't cheer me up. I flew to California for the holidays, our first Christmas without Uncle Hal.

"I may be leaving Japan soon," I told my family when I left.

"Have you finished your job already?" my father asked.

"Just about," I said. There didn't seem much point in trying to explain that I hadn't even begun my job. The concept of "insufficiently firm enhancements" is not easy to convey to the older generation.

Back in Tokyo, I treated Miyuki and Yoz to dinner in a French restaurant, and Ikeda joined us. It wasn't possible to avoid seafood altogether, but my meal of broccoli aspic with red pepper sauce, sole stuffed with sea urchins and shrimp, and red-wine sorbet was *oishii* (delicious). A few days later, Miyuki and Yoz gave me a birthday gift, a beautiful cup and saucer. "*Tsumaranai mono desu ga*," they murmured, in the approved Japanese manner. "It's just a little thing."

I celebrated my birthday by having friends over for dinner: the Colemans, Ken Matsuda, his wife, Debby, and their eighteen-month-old son, Rory, who was just learning how to walk. "Hi!" he would say, tottering up to you and waving his chubby little hands in the air. "Bye!" he would add, tottering away.

I made soup, a pasta dish, and a big salad. My guests brought gifts, cards, long-stemmed roses, a bottle of wine, two baskets of strawberries, cream for the berries, and a chocolate cake with HAPPY BIRTHDAY NANO on it. The cake was covered with chocolate sprinkles, which flew in all directions when I blew out the candles. Rory, meanwhile, had gathered all my cushions together and started stacking them up.

"Rory-*chan*, what are you doing?" asked Tessa.

"Make cake for R'annon!" answered the industrious toddler.

Thirty-eight! I had never intended to get older than thirty. I hadn't been paying attention, obviously. I'd got distracted, and the years had crept up on me. One night, lying sleepless in my tatami-mat room, I found wrinkles in my wrists. Wrinkles in my face, slight ones, I was accustomed to—but in my wrists? My hair, a dark red-brown when I moved to Tokyo, was now streaked with white. This was probably happening right on schedule, but I was more than willing to blame Japan, Hewlett-Packard, the Semiconductor Productivity Network, and Ebisu himself for these signs of aging.

For the first time in my life, as I lay looking at my wrinkled wrists, I took on board the fact that there was going to be, in my case, no special dispensation. Like everyone else, I was going to get old and eventually die. A haunting moment for each of us, that first intimation of mortality. Mine was accompanied by the frantic barking of dogs and the whine of the *bōsōzoku* boys.

A few days later, Ken invited me out to lunch. *This is it*, I thought gloomily. *So much for a suitcase stuffed with money.* Oh, I had *some* money, I hadn't been totally profligate, but not a suitcase full. More like a large wallet.

Ken loved Japanese food, but generously deferred to my tastes and took me to the coffee shop across the street from the office, where I ordered a hamburger and a chocolate milkshake. Impeccable as always in a suit and tie, my new boss regarded me sympathetically. "So, Rhiannon, I guess you haven't started on Ebisu yet."

"I'm still waiting for the word from Duncan. I did rewrite the specs."

"Yes, I thought they seemed unusually readable."

"Thanks. There was nothing else to do."

"It must be awfully boring."

"It is." (But lucrative!)

"How's your book coming?"

"Badly."

"I guess it's hard to write about Palo Alto when you're stuck in Tokyo."

"It is."

"And now that SPN is obsolete, things are even more difficult."

He's trying to make me feel better, I thought. It wasn't working. The waitress brought our food. My hamburger tasted like cardboard. What did the Japanese feed their cattle—obsolete documentation? I gave up after a few bites and devoted myself to the milkshake.

"Well, Rhiannon," said my new boss, "I know you may not like this, but hear me out, okay?"

I sucked up the last of my drink and braced myself.

"HPJ would like you to stay for another year, if you can stand it," Ken said. Then he gave me the biggest pay raise of my life.

From up in the Japanese pantheon, where he lives with the gods of Irony, Paradox, and Circuitously Fulfilled Ambition, Ebisu winked at me.

Seventeen

"NOT BE!"

Ebisu lived! Although the SPN product line was "mature," our existing customers, having invested expensively in our products, were still keen to buy the enhancements. In late January, nine months after I'd moved to Japan, Duncan told me that the code was firm enough for documentation. Energetically, I started writing field descriptions. "The number of wafers reworked or rejected because of the corresponding cause code . . . Specifies a metrology machine's data-report identifier . . . If DOWN-LOAD=Y and the present recipe is the one already downloaded, a different recipe will not be downloaded . . ."

Ken and Debby, a striking blue-eyed blonde, gave a party for the SPN group at their four-bedroom house in Mitaka. Through this immense space wandered the Tomodachi, not quite concealing their amazement at the amount of room that Westerners seem to require. Although the Matsudas, with help from Tessa, had prepared a lavish spread, what our colleagues enjoyed most was watching Debby use the garbage disposal. They'd never seen one. Disposals are a luxury in a city where garbage is collected four times a week. (And you could leave

out anything: rusty old bicycles, dysfunctional hairdryers, discarded nipple-covers . . .)

Having grown used to my scaled-down model, I was more
impressed with the refrigerator. An entire Japanese village could
have lived in it. And you could roast a turkey in the Matsudas'
oven. I could only fit a couple of chicken breasts in mine, and
then only if the chicken hadn't taken anything bigger than a B-
cup.

As the Japanese clustered in the kitchen with the garbage
disposal, Rory Kentaro Matsuda romped through the huge
rooms, break-dancing and then applauding himself, telling complete strangers that he loved them, and calling everyone
"Matsuda." Rory believed, or perhaps I mean knew, that we all
belong to the same family.

It's never too early to introduce children to Shakespeare, so
I decided to teach him Hamlet's famous soliloquy. Rory loved
it. Every time I started, "To be or not to be," he bellowed, "NOT
BE!"

Our colleagues were even more amazed by Rory than by
the garbage disposal. Your typical Japanese infant is born in a
condition of tranquillity that an American couldn't achieve after a lifetime spent sniffing incense and meditating in the lotus
position. If it gets wet or cold or hungry, the infant will cough
discreetly to attract its mother's attention. In the grip of severe
pain, it may go so far as to whimper, but the lads had never
heard anything like the full-throated yells that emerged from
young Rory.

"Excuse me, Rhiannon-*san*," said the Imp, who had been
elected spokesman for the lads. "We would like to ask this question, please. Is Rory-*chan* a normal American child?"

"Oh, no," I replied. "He's much more adorable."

"Adorable? *Wakarimasen*. (I don't understand.)"

"Adorable. Cute. *Kawaii desu*."

"*Ah sō desu ka!*" said the Imp.

The Tomodachi were beginning to understand why Americans require such large houses.

On March 5, Bob Dylan and Tom Petty played at the Budokan in the Imperial Palace gardens. Yoz got tickets for the Colemans and himself and me. The Budokan was packed with baby-boomer *gaijin* for whom the concert was a wallow in nostalgia. I started crying as soon as Dylan opened his mouth. Crying meant I had to keep blowing my nose—and with Yoz sitting beside me!—but it couldn't be helped. Dylan's high nasal voice had wrapped itself like a ribbon around the gift of growing up in the sixties, with all their excitement and promise. It struck my ears now as a lament for frustrated dreams.

Earlier, I'd gone with Miyuki to a Stevie Wonder concert, a much less charged experience. I had accepted Miyuki's invitation with misgivings. At the last rock concert I'd attended, Rod Stewart at the Cow Palace in San Francisco, my friend Tricia and I were seated behind a passed-out teenage girl. Her boyfriend French-kissed her for several minutes and then wandered down to the dance floor. The girl slept through several songs, but as Rod launched into "Twisting the Night Away," she woke up, stumbled out into the aisle, vomited, and fell headlong down the concrete steps onto her heavily pregnant belly. I held her and wiped her face while Tricia ran down to the dance floor to retrieve the boyfriend.

"She needs a doctor," we urged.

"No way, man," he replied. "Happens all the time."

At a Japanese rock concert, no one was drunk or drugged. No one yelled, screamed, snorted, toked, injected, or threw up. When Stevie sat on the edge of the stage to sing "I Just Called to Say I Love You"—a huge hit in Japan; the electronics shops in Kichijoji had been playing it for weeks—the audience sang softly along with him. When he launched into "Superstition," heads turned all over the auditorium as the audience consulted itself. Agreement was reached, and the young people stood up, all at the same time, and grooved gently to the music. When the song ended, they clapped enthusiastically but decorously, and then, in unison, sat down again.

"*Sugoi desu ne!*" I said.

"Yes, Stevie is great," Miyuki said.

I hadn't meant Stevie, actually. I'd meant the audience.

I was beginning to understand why the Japanese can live harmoniously together in such small houses.

The Colemans were almost ready to "repatriate." Before they left, Yoz invited them to spend ten days touring Kyūshū, the southernmost of Japan's three main islands, with himself, his sister, and one of his cousins. "I think it will be so *nice* if you come too," he told me.

There were several arguments against this plan.

(1) I was supposed to be documenting Ebisu.
(2) I had come to Japan to save money, not to spend it.
(3) Peculiar seafood would be involved.

But there were also arguments in favor.

(1) Ebisu was obsolete. Kyūshū wasn't.
(2) Money be damned.
(3) I could always eat rice.

But the most persuasive argument was that Yoz would make all the arrangements. Travel in Japan is not spontaneous. You don't just decide, "I think I'll fly down to Kyūshū for a week," and go. You plan your trip weeks or months in advance, and then you visit a travel agent, disclose your plans, wait while the necessary reservations are made, and pay the agent—in cash; they don't accept credit cards—who passes your money along to the railway company and hotels. No one had been able to find a bilingual travel agency. The Colemans used a place in

Kichijoji where simple English was understood, and I'd gone there to make reservations for my trip to Nikko. It had taken two hours and left me weak with remorse for making the staff work so hard.

Those hours in the travel agency had demonstrated to me, once and for all, that I had the wrong temperament to make a success of living in Japan. An optimistic extrovert was called for, a passion-flower like Tessa who bloomed in exuberant indifference to the impression she was making, not a thin-skinned shrinking violet like myself. Confronted with a rude Parisian waiter, I could rise to the challenge and assert myself. What the hell, I wasn't going to hurt *his* feelings. But the Japanese, so eager to serve, so worried about failing in their duties, made me feel guilty, for how could they serve me properly when I couldn't speak their language?

Here again Tessa had the edge. I wouldn't say anything unless I could say it perfectly, so I spoke Japanese only when Mrs. Yamaguchi made me. Tessa, on the other hand, burbled away, no doubt mangling the language as winningly as she mangled English—at a dinner party recently, she had asked one of the American guests, an editor, for a "prescription" to his magazine—but nevertheless communicating. She didn't worry about making it impossible for people to perform their *nimmu* or saddling them unintentionally with *on*, any more than Duncan and Linette worried about making reservations for weekend trips to the country.

"Oh, we've been stranded a few times on spur-of-the-moment trips, but it always works out," Linette said cheerfully.

"That's right," Duncan agreed. "Last weekend we couldn't find the restaurant we wanted, but we found a great sushi bar instead."

It was clear that both the Colemans and the Marshalls were better than I was at adapting to Japan. If the question was, "To be or not to be—in Japan," Rory had the right answer for me: "Not be!" This was a disheartening realization given that I had just agreed to spend another year in Tokyo. More to distract myself from thinking about this than because I had any burning desire to see Kyūshū, I agreed to go with Yoz and the Colemans to the southern island.

Eighteen

THE MAGIC GORGE

In a place called Takachiho, the River Gokase has spent the past several centuries cutting its way through flows of lava from a nearby volcano. The sides of the resulting gorge are steep and gray, like the walls of an English cathedral, and topped with groves of ferns and trees. At the bottom of the gorge runs the river, the color of melted jade, with small boats floating on it like jewels.

The Takachiho gorge is said to be magic: it's the place where a goddess performed the world's first dance. Every winter, in the town, a dance called the *Iwato-kagura* is staged in celebration. In March 1986, Paul and Tessa and I got to see it. We walked through the town in the frosty dark, making clouds in the air with our breath, to a hall where people were kneeling on tatami-mat floors under a beamed wood ceiling. The stage was decorated with young trees and paper banners. The crowd was convivial, happy to be there, and when they spotted us foreigners at the back, they smiled.

During our first few days on Kyūshū, we had visited a shrine carved into a cave and a beach covered with striated slabs of hard gray lava. In a rustic beamed restaurant with a grandfather clock and tables made from thick slabs of polished wood, we'd slurped *tempura soba* from pottery bowls. Later, I'd watched my skin turn shrimp-pink in the hot tub at our *ryokan*.

Still to come were more memorable Kyūshū experiences. I would stand with my friends on the snow-covered top of Mount Aso, the gorge's volcanic parent, listening to icy winds howl like Japanese devils out of the enormous crater. I would meet Yoz's eighty-nine-year-old grandmother, who had never seen a Westerner before, and drink sake out of a bamboo pole. In a *ryokan* in Beppu, I would watch Yoz eat "dancing fish": tiny transparent creatures that swim around in your bowl like animated toothpicks. You pour vinegar on them to slow them down a bit, and then tip them down your throat. "They dance all the way down," Yoz explained. "Please *enjoy* the pleasurable sensation."

Tonight, though, we were in Takachiho, waiting for the goddess to dance.

"In the beginning," says Genesis, "God created the heaven and the earth. And the earth was without form, and void; and darkness was upon the face of the deep."

In the beginning, agree the sacred books of Shinto, the earth was without form, and void; and darkness was upon the face of the deep. But milling about in the darkness were divine spirits called *kami*. Two of them, a brother and sister, stirred the ocean with a spear ("And the Spirit of God moved upon the face of the waters," says Genesis). The ocean thickened; the spear dripped; and the droplet turned into an island, the first island of the Inland Sea. ("And God said, Let the waters under the heaven be gathered together unto one place, and let the dry land appear: and it was so.")

So far, both traditions agree: divinity makes a home for us out of the sea. But then the traditions diverge. We inheritors of Judaism and Christianity get Adam and Eve, the forbidden fruit, the insinuating serpent, eviction from Paradise—the woman's fault, and she is duly punished: ". . . in sorrow thou shalt bring forth children; and thy desire shall be to thy husband, and he shall rule over thee."

Clothed in coats of skins, the first couple are driven from the garden so they won't become immortal (" . . . lest he put forth his hand, and take also of the tree of life, and eat, and live for ever"). They begin tilling the soil. Sin and sorrow. Death and the corruption of the flesh. Orders, dictated to Moses, involving the preparation of food, the sacrifice of animals, and the covering up of holy objects with the skins of badgers. Blessings, curses. Exile. A flood. And finally, thirty-nine Biblical books and a chapter of begats later, the Holy Ghost appears to a woman named Mary. "And she shall bring forth a son, and thou shalt call his name Jesus: for he shall save his people from their sins."

He would have seemed a sad figure to the ancient Japanese, our God, all alone in the firmament, with no village, no family, no one else in the world like him. If He behaved capriciously, if He burdened his people with commandments engraved in stone, if He let them die into oblivion for generations and then, relenting, created a Son to give them eternal life (and keep Him company in heaven)—*ah, sō desu ne!* That is understandable.

The Shinto heaven, by contrast, swarms with inhabitants. The spear-wielding brother and sister, Izanagi and Izanami, make love—this is not a sin, for no one is offended by it—and she gives birth to the eight islands of Japan, plus assorted divinities. An ungrateful son, the God of Fire, burns her to death. Izanagi goes to the underworld and finds her in terrible shape, rotten and full of evil spirits. Death hasn't agreed with her, and she's furious at being seen in her condition. She sets devils on her brother. He escapes and stuffs a rock in the entrance to hell.

What does he do next? If he were an English god, he'd make a nice cup of tea. But he's a Japanese god, so he takes a bath. His discarded clothes turn into *kami*. More *kami* emerge from his nose and eyes, including another brother-sister pair, the Impetuous Male (*Susano wo*) and the Goddess of Light (*Amaterasu-omi-kami*), the ancestress of the imperial family and most revered of all the *kami*.

The Impetuous Male is given the Earth to govern. Living up to his name, he causes so much trouble that his offended sister hides in a cave. Once again, there is darkness upon the face of the deep.

The *kami* gather to discuss the situation. How is the Goddess of Light to be winkled out of her cave? They ask the God of Thought for advice. He has lots of ideas, none of them practicable. (There's someone like him in every committee meeting.) And then the Goddess of Laughter takes over. She performs a sacred dance and gets so carried away that she lifts up her skirts. As the *kami* howl with laughter, the Goddess in the cave pokes her head out to see what's so funny.

Let there be light.

The dancers moved onto the stage, robed in white, wearing elaborate masks: red-faced *kami*, bird-faced *kami*, beautiful white-faced *kami*. As flutes and drums played tuneless, eerie music, they struck poses and made stylized gestures. The audience clapped and chuckled. These were user-friendly gods, gods who made mistakes, gods you could laugh with. I watched and pondered the distance between their heaven and the heaven I was raised to believe in, where God sits in solitary glory, judging the souls of men.

After the ceremony, the priest of the Iwato Shrine, who was acquainted with Yoz's cousin, invited us to have tea with him. We sat on tatami mats around a *kotatsu*, which counts as one of the great Japanese inventions: a table with a heater underneath and a skirt attached to the edges. With our legs tucked under the priest's table, we were warm and cozy, although we Americans had the usual trouble sitting still. The walls of his study were lined, comfortingly, with books.

For more than an hour, with Yoz interpreting, we asked questions and the priest answered. He was a slight, soft-spoken man with collar-length black hair combed straight back from a high forehead. He had a dangerous face, noble, spiritual, intelligent. You'd believe anything from a face like that.

His wife came in with a tray and set down a pot of tea and white bowls full of plump red strawberries. She didn't join us, but bowed and smiled, with her hand over her mouth in the shy way of Japanese women, and then retreated to the kitchen or some other part of the house. We drank tea, ate strawberries, and listened to the priest. I should have asked if I could take notes but I was lulled into silence. The priest's Japanese rang strangely in my ears. He was making the language, which had always struck me as monotonous, sound beautiful.

"A preacher ought to be good-looking," wrote Sei Shōnagon in her *Pillow Book*, a classic of Japanese literature from the tenth century. "For, if we are properly to understand his worthy sentiments, we must keep our eyes on him while he speaks . . ." I kept my eyes on the priest. I couldn't understand his words, but I thought that they were leading me somewhere.

Next morning, I got up early, skipped the white-rice-and-green-tea breakfast at our *ryokan*, and walked alone through the town to the Iwato Shrine. As I passed under the plain, unpainted *torii*, the noise of the town faded. All I could hear was birdsong and another sound, soft and whiskery. I came to a clearing of sunny earth, striped with the shadows of huge cryptomeria trees. The priest was there, framed between a pair of brown-wood buildings, wearing a full-sleeved white shirt, long dark purple skirt, and sandals. With a wood-and-straw broom, he was sweeping up leaves.

The night before, I'd been a spectator at a ritual from an ancient, unfamiliar world. Now here was that same world, walked off the stage: actual, present, existing in the same time as my world of e-mail and deadlines and bank accounts, a world in which, free of faith and tradition, I believe in nothing but myself. It seemed to me, as I stood in tree shadow, that if I stepped into the sunlight I could move from my world into this one. I could be like Yoz and have ancestors following me. I could live among gods.

It lasted for about forty seconds and it wasn't like being in a trance. It was as if I'd been in a trance all along and had suddenly been awakened. I saw that the leaves had veins like mine. I felt the birdsong as if I were singing it. I couldn't tell where my body stopped and the air began. I heard the Buddha say, "All three worlds are my home, all the creatures in this house are my children."

I stepped out into sunlight that was as warm as my blood.

I'll never know what should have happened next. Maybe it was what *did* happen: my friends came walking through the *torii*, bringing my world with them. "Hey, Nano, we thought we'd lost you!" Tessa said, slipping her arm through mine.

"We never *expected* to find you here," Yoz said.

The priest walked up to us, smiling, and spoke to Yoz.

"He says we must *walk* around the *trees*," Yoz translated, pointing to a pair of cryptomeria that were linked by a straw rope. "Because whoever walks around the *trees* together will always be *united*."

So we joined hands and circled the trees: Paul and his wife, Tessa; Yoz and his sister and cousin; the priest of the Iwato Shrine; and me.

Something must have gone wrong with the magic. Afterward, I didn't feel any more united to the people I'd walked around the tree with than I had before. But I left a part of my heart in the place.

Nineteen

DEATH BY PHILODENDRON

It was harder than ever to return to Tokyo. The city was a monstrous growth that covered the earth, trees, flowers, rivers, and my spirits. Her multi-story buildings jabbed into the sky like upraised fingers. In their shadow, her people toiled like—surely I could find a more original simile than "ants"?

I couldn't. And the fact that most of the ants were glad to be living in Tokyo didn't alter my opinion that we'd all be happier out in the country, living a simple life close to Nature, listening to birdsong and sweeping up leaves and, well, doing whatever else it is that people do out in the country. "When a man is tired of London," said Samuel Johnson, "he is tired of life." The Japanese feel the same way about their capital, but in my opinion, when a woman is tired of Tokyo, she is probably just tired of Tokyo.

As winter blew and rained its way toward spring, my mood darkened like the pall of smoke in our office. "Curiouser and curiouser," I wrote to the Thompsons. "IIP has 'matured' our product line. If Paul and Duncan hadn't come to Japan, the Semiconductor Productivity Network would be dead. As it is, the

165

products have struggled out of their coffin and walk among us, obsolete, badly documented and unsupportable, but revenant: The Software That Would Not Die! A group of 'freshmen,'* most of them smokers, has joined us, and Ken and Ikeda are busy selling our cobweb-covered code in Korea and Taiwan. A French company is also interested. (*Le SPN! Les softwares très networkâbles pour faire meilleur votre productivité . . .*)

"Duncan's team has decided to 'enhance the functionality'; i.e., change the Ebisu software so it won't work the way I've just finished saying it does. My documentation is obsolete before it's left the building. It's also in English, which from now on will *not* be the native language of any of our customers. Yet they want me to stay on and write more. My God, what a racket!"

The foreign, exciting at first and then briefly familiar, began to turn strange. Things I'd shrugged off in my enthusiasm for new experiences started to rankle. Murder and robbery are rare in Japan, but every day, on crowded trains all over the country, thousands of girls and young women endure in silence the groping fingers of male passengers, while schoolboys and salary-men leaf through comic-book depictions of violent pornography. (After glancing at a boy's *manga* on the train to Shibuya and seeing an illustration of a girl with a gun's nozzle stuck up her vagina, I never looked at one again.)** Even the newspapers and magazines on display in the HPJ lobby contained pictures of naked women.†

---

* Young men of twenty-two and twenty-three, beginning their careers at HPJ. As is usual in Japan, they were all hired during the same period, went through orientation together, and started work on the same day.
** *Manga* cater to many tastes; not all are pornographic.
† A 1998 survey found that one in seven women working in Japanese Government offices reported being pressured into a sexual relationship with male colleagues. And according to an AP article in January, 1999, one in every five women in the Self Defense Forces said she had either been asked or forced to have sex with senior officers or colleagues. Another form of harassment reported by the military women: being required to serve tea.

Brooding over these and past injustices, such as the "Grand-mother-Throwing-Away Mountain" near Nagano where legend holds that old women used to be left to die, I reminded myself that the U.S. has its own kinds of sexism, some of them deadly. It is perhaps not surprising that this failed to improve my spirits.

In Tokyo, the noise seemed louder, the air dirtier, the crowds thicker. My "petals on a wet black bough" mantra didn't help much any more. The language remained incomprehensible no matter how many verbs I memorized.* There were so many minor earthquakes that the ground seemed to be trembling continuously under my feet. There were bigger earthquakes too. One afternoon, when I was eating lunch in the coffee shop across the street from the office, the building began to shake. A plant in a macramé hanger started swinging crazily over my head and everyone looked at me to see how the *gaijin* would react. I went on sipping my milkshake, feigning indifference while headlines wrote themselves across my mind.

> Falling Philodendron Kills American, 38
> "She died with a hamburger in her hand"

I had started to see myself through Japanese eyes. A trim size six in those days, I had been accustomed to thinking of myself as slender. Now I felt like a hulk, towering over men and women alike. My body was flagrant, bulgy, out of control. My skin looked as if it had been bleached, my feet were too big, my nose was too long, my hips were too wide, and my hair could not be cut into submission even by a stylist who had trained at Vidal Sassoon in London and spoke English with a Japanese-Cockney accent. "Your hair doesn't hoff glow quick-ree," he

---

* "In Japanese," Yoz tried to explain, "the verbs are changed into five moods: the beforehand mood, the mood able to be connected to a verb, the original mood, the mood used as adjective, the supposing mood, and the imperative mood." Striking a reassuring note, he added, "This is very difficult to understand."

said, meaning that my hair doesn't half grow quickly. It was an admission of defeat, similar to admissions I'd heard in varying accents from hairstylists all over the world, but I went to him anyway because during the shampoo he massaged my scalp for fifteen minutes. In Japan that was as close as I was going to get to sex.

Below my thatch of weed-like hair, my glasses, thick as bottle bottoms, sat like a windshield across my thin little face. When I got back to California, I would switch to contact lenses. I would also use my relocation allowance to get my teeth straightened, transforming myself, in the space of one year, from a plain woman into an attractive one. Even my hair would redeem itself, or perhaps it's more accurate to say that fashion has finally caught up with my hair. But all that was in the future. For now I was in Tokyo, a frumpy beast surrounded by diminutive doll-like beauties.

I grew more and more self-conscious. When I boarded a train, if there were any seats at all, the other passengers would move *way over* to make room for me. Did I smell bad? I had read somewhere that the old Japanese term for "foreigner" was "stinks like butter." Had this been updated to "stinks like pizza"? Or was it my size? "Attention, fellow passengers! Large foreign buttocks approaching!"

I kept willing myself to be smaller, pulling bones together, contracting muscles. My body lodged its protests. I'd never had back pain before, but that winter, when I had to stand for any length of time, my lower back would begin to cramp as if a fist were clenching inside. By the time I left Tokyo, I couldn't walk for more than twenty minutes without ending up in agony. Like the trees, like the dogs in Nishi Eifuku, I was being bonsai'd.

I felt feverish all the time. I was so irate about the cigarette smoke (with attendant sore throat and stinging eyes) that I had to restrain myself from ripping the foul objects out of my colleagues' mouths. One afternoon before my Japanese class, I started crying in the ladies' room at work because I hadn't found time to study the lesson.

These were physical manifestations of a spiritual malaise. The vision I'd had in the Iwato Shrine stayed with me: there was another world and I belonged in it, not here; and by "here" I didn't mean Tokyo. I meant my job, my culture, my whole damned life. It wasn't as simple as wanting to live in a Shinto shrine and it wasn't new. I'd had it always, this misfit, stuck-outside-the-wall feeling. Technical writer, scholar of English literature, British Merchant Navy wife, clerk-typist, sorority girl, dutiful middle-class daughter. So many roles, and none of them was right for me. For thirty-eight years I'd been auditioning for my life, and I still didn't have the part. I wasn't even sure which part I wanted.

Under this uncertainty lay deeper doubts, engendered by my months in Japan, about the nature of identity itself. How much of "me" was me and how much was culture? If I hadn't been born American, would I still be restless, ambitious, con-trary-minded? Could the same raw material, worked upon by a different society, have produced a tea-making office lady or a contented housewife? How could I know who I was? How could anyone know who she was? There are people who don't ask themselves questions like these and they're undoubtedly hap-pier than I am, but I have never known how to stop asking.

The night of the earthquake at the Century Hyatt Hotel, I hadn't been sure what frightened me more: being different or finding out that I didn't feel different at all. I had worried about what British Empire builders used to call "going native." I'd been afraid that I would lose myself. But although Japan im-pressed me, she didn't tempt me. I wasn't going native, but I was losing myself anyway.

At night in the House of Clear Water, I would put on ear-phones and listen to Bruce Springsteen, whose raw American voice had the power to make me feel, temporarily, as if I had roots. Sometimes I stood on my balcony and shook my fist at the *bōsōzoku* boys, although I knew they couldn't see me. No one in Japan could see me, for how could I explain to these successful, hard-working, cooperative people my life-long search for an authentic self? I felt grossly in evidence and at the same time invisible.

My parents were Methodists. Understandably, they wanted their children to be Methodists too. To this aim they took us to Sunday school, church, and summer Bible camp. At some point when I was around eight years old, the teachings stopped making sense to me, but I didn't feel able to refuse church-going until my mid-teens. Dressed up in my Sunday-best frock and patent-leather shoes, listening to the minister read from the Bible, I would think: I am the only person here who doesn't believe this. Terrifyingly, the church would seem to waver, as if the whole edifice, the altar, the pews, the minister, the suited men, the hatted-and-gloved women, the children squirming and kicking their heels, would disappear at any moment with my parents and my little sister, leaving me alone forever.

It was happening again now. HPJ was the church, software was the religion, and my colleagues were the congregation, living by a set of beliefs that I couldn't share. "This is what makes you feel so isolated," I told myself. "It's not because you're living in Tokyo. If you were hanging out with Japanese writers and artists, you'd probably feel right at home—at least until the octopus was served." I thanked all seven Happy Gods on a daily basis for Yoz, who made me feel less isolated because he seemed to share some of the same feelings.

But Yoz couldn't cure what ailed me. Nor could Ken and Debby or the rest of the Tomodachi. Every morning as the sky lightened over Nishi Eifuku and I dragged myself out of bed after a few hours' sleep, I would tell myself that I couldn't bear Tokyo any longer; I had to get out. But I was through pretending, as I had until now, that money didn't matter. Wasn't it because I didn't have money that I had to keep submitting myself to experiences like this? The longer I stayed in Japan, the more money I'd save. The more money I saved, the more control I'd have over my life. The more control I had over my life, the happier I'd be. Therefore I should stay in Japan as long as I could, even though it was making me miserable because I had no control over my life. If there was a flaw in this logic I was too tired to see it.

So I stayed up late at night, shivering on my balcony. It faced east, toward the Pacific Ocean, toward California, which was, I kept trying to reassure myself, the direction of home.

THE REMAINS
OF THE STAY

{}

Spring begins again;
Upon folly,
Folly returns.
—Issa

Twenty

用
川

BURT'S FINAL FLING

The cherry trees flowered on the southern island. At his shrine by the magic gorge, the priest would soon be sweeping up paper-thin pink blossoms as well as leaves. The "*sakura* front" moved north toward Tokyo, the branches of the trees on my lane turned lumpy with buds, and baby ducks popped up again on the lake at Inokashira Park.

The SPN group had started two new projects. One was a second set of software enhancements that the lads named "Benten" after the Goddess of Love. I would start documenting Benten as soon as I finished with Ebisu. The other project was our farewell party for the Colemans. Our Master of Ceremonies was Yoshioka, one of the freshmen, sleepy-eyed behind his heavy tortoise-shell specs. I promptly nicknamed him "M.C." Spats was Party Consultant and Performance Manager. Miyuki and I were Project Managers. Our code name for the project, M.C. revealed in an e-mail message, was MIAOU CAT. It was never clear to me why we needed a code name, but there's no doubt that MIAOU CAT is a good one.

In a series of after-hours meetings, we decided that the party would be held in a private room in a restaurant in Kichijoji. Miyuki would put together an album of photographs illustrating Paul and Tessa's two years in Japan. Various SPN members would give performances that involved singing, playing musical instruments, yelling, and demonstrating karate kicks. Untalented in all these ways, I offered to write new lyrics for the all-too-familiar tune of "I Just Called to Say I Love You," which I could lead in a sing-along. Spats, who had heard me sing, instantly offered to accompany me on his guitar. "I can play loudly," he assured Miyuki. Money was set aside for a gift that I agreed to buy at Tessa's favorite pottery shop in Mitaka.

But it wasn't enough. Not for Paul and Tessa. The MIAOU CAT team sat looking at me hopefully, evincing a touching though ordinarily misguided faith in my abilities as a party-planner. Inspired, I ran to my cubicle and came back holding Tessa's plastic lizard. "I think," I told my colleagues, "that Paul-*san* and Tessa-*san* would enjoy it very much if someone came to their party dressed like Burt."

Everyone agreed that this was a *subarashii*—wonderful—idea. Everyone thanked me very much for contributing so creatively to MIAOU CAT. Everyone decided that Spats would make a perfect Burt-impersonator. Everyone then placed the job of creating a man-sized Australian frilled lizard costume squarely in my lap.

Undaunted, I enlisted Yoz to help me—in a rash moment he had told me that he could sew—and we set a date to go shopping for fabric. But Miyuki took pity on me; or perhaps she feared that Nakamura-*san* and I, brilliant though we undoubtedly were, would be unequal to the task of fashioning anything that looked remotely like Burt. She had a friend, it turned out, who worked for a Japanese television company, and the television company just happened to have, lying around in a drawer, an Australian frilled lizard costume made out of rubber, which they would gladly lend to us for our farewell party.

I was deeply impressed. If you called up an American network affiliate and asked if you could borrow their Australian frilled lizard costume, I bet you anything they'd say, "No way." And your local public television station, because of budget cuts, would have auctioned off their Australian frilled lizard costume and would have nothing to offer you except a glove puppet of Kermit the Frog.

While the MIAOU CAT committee continued its top-secret preparations, Paul and Tessa were treated to a flock of smaller parties. Ken and Debby gave a dinner party at their house and served lasagna. I gave a dinner party in a Mexican restaurant and drank so many Sangrias that I fell asleep on the train back to Nishi Eifuku. Ken and Debby gave a second dinner party in a Swiss restaurant on the fiftieth floor of a Shinjuku skyscraper, during which the Matsudas and I got to practice our Japanese on the French waiter and our French on the Japanese waiter, owing to our inability to switch languages fast enough. Christine Yamada and her husband, Kanji, who also worked for HPJ, gave a party at their house in Mitakadai and invited the entire SPN group.

Miyuki gave a kimono party. The guests were Paul and Tessa, Easy Rider, Spats, and me. Miyuki's mother and grandmother welcomed us to their comfortable house in Akishimashi. In suitable surroundings—wood-paneled walls, *shoji* screens, tatami-mat floors—Paul and Tessa donned traditional Japanese dress: a dark blue robe for Paul; a turquoise, orange, and white kimono for Tessa. In my photograph of the event, Paul looks uncomfortable and Tessa looks demure, which must have been the effect of the kimono. Miyuki's handsome mother and grandmother, the latter elegantly clad in a shimmering lavender kimono, looked on with laughter.

MIAOU CAT day was fast approaching. M.C. was heroically memorizing whole paragraphs of English. Copies of my lyrics were distributed. When Paul and Tessa were out, everyone went around muttering, "We just want—to say—we'll miss you. We just want—to say we really care . . ."

On the morning of the party, a Wednesday, I stunned the Tomodachi by getting to work at eight-thirty in order to rehearse the song with Spats. To record this event for posterity, Spats whipped out his camera and took a photo of me standing baggy-eyed under the clock.

It was a foul day, windy and raining. This was tough on Spats, who had to take the train east after work to pick up his costume at the TV studio, and then lug the bulky thing in a huge plastic bag all the way to Kichijoji. He arrived at the restaurant soaked with rain. As he climbed the stairs, with Miyuki and me waiting anxiously at the top, the bag trailed after him like a collapsed parachute.

After the talent show, Spats picked up his guitar and I led the song. It made Paul cry, although that could have been my singing. While Paul dried his eyes, Spats slipped out of the room and I announced that a special guest had asked if he could join the party.

"Bruce Springsteen!" Tessa cried. (I'd told her I would try to book him.)

"No, Tessa, it's someone who loves you, someone who owes you everything. But you may not recognize him, because he's got a lot bigger . . ." I gestured with my hands. "As you know, you have that effect on men." We'd all had plenty to drink, so this was received uproariously.

Miyuki held the door open and Spats waddled in, unrecognizable, completely encased in yellow and green rubber. He had a bright red mouth, black eyes on top of his head, a long swishing tail, and an enormous frill.

"Burt!" Tessa shrieked.

Everyone was laughing. Even Ito-san was laughing. One of the freshmen laughed so hard that he fell off his chair, which made everyone laugh even harder. Burt was the hit of the party.

Next day, egged on by Ikeda—who decided, wisely, that if you've scored an Australian frilled lizard costume, you might as well make the most of it—Spats dressed up like Burt again and paraded through the Takaido office, wearing a sash that read, in big optimistic letters, SURVIVAL SPN. You'd think he'd have been annoyed about having to impersonate a large foreign reptile, but Spats sent me an e-mail message, thanking me for my "so nice ideas for that party, one after another." And M.C. wrote to me as well.

> The last night party was great successful. I thinked "What a fantastic night." Thank you from the bottom of my heart for your contributions to the party. I think our cooperation make the party so fantastic.

As always, or so it seemed, my feelings were more compli-cated. I loved Paul and Tessa and I was glad that MIAOU CAT had done them proud, but I was relieved that they were leaving. My friendship with Tessa had been strained for months. Her habit of seeming able to read my mind was unnerving. To give one example, I'd composed a poem for her 30th birthday, "The San-Jue Blues" (*san-jue* is Japanese for "thirty"). I wrote it on the computer at work (bad girl!) and encrypted it. There's no way Tessa should have known it was there, let alone been able to read it, but a few days before her birthday, before I'd even printed the poem, she turned to me and said, "Oh Nano—I have the '*san-jue* blues.'" And then she looked at me knowingly, as if daring me to challenge her. Where had she picked up that phrase? Was she snooping through my computer files? It seemed like the kind of thing she might do, especially if she suspected that my feelings for her and Paul had been compromised. Or was I imagining things? Either the woman who shared my cu-bicle was spying on me, or I was turning paranoid. Neither one was a happy prospect.

The underlying (or as Tessa would have said, "underlining") problem was the pressure I felt to demonstrate an unconditional loyalty to the Colemans, while trying to maintain a good working relationship with someone whom they perceived as an enemy.

As for Paul, bless him, I've never had a manager who was more determined to be unimpressed by my achievements. It's true that he didn't see me achieve much, but was that my fault? It's not as though I kept a voodoo doll labeled "Ebisu" in my desk and kept sticking pins in it. I wanted work; anything was better than sitting in that damned cubicle breathing cigarette smoke for no good reason. I begged for work, and when anyone gave me some, I fell upon it with glad cries. But then, dilemma. If I blazed through the task with my customary dispatch (I type fast, remember, almost as fast as Fingers), I'd be sitting there with nothing to do again. If I worked slowly, Paul would think I was dawdling.

The trouble with having invested too much in being an A student is that there's always a report card in your head. In Tokyo, mine was full of F's. The Japanese language, feud-resolving, creative writing, sophisticated world traveling—I was failing every test. And here was Paul, whose opinions I respected, acting like a disappointed teacher.

In California, I assumed, the Colemans and I would meet again and resume our friendship over a bottle or two of Dry Creek Valley Zinfandel. In the meantime, I was glad to see them go.

Aside from the Marshalls, I was undoubtedly the only person who was. Paul and Tessa had come to Japan as strangers, but more than a dozen of the Tomodachi drove to Narita, a four-hour round trip, to say goodbye.

Twenty-One

". . . MUST BE HAMMERED DOWN."

As soon as Paul's heels cleared the door, hordes of boiler-suited men swarmed into our office and started taking it apart.

A power struggle had been going on between the SPN group and the group in the next room, the GINR. (Ken and I decided that this stood for "Give In Now, Rebels!") While Paul was with us the GINR members were kept at bay, cowed into submission behind their wall. The day after Paul left, the wall, quite literally, came down. So did the partitions that Paul had fought so hard to have erected around our cubicles. Japanese managers don't hold with partitions. They like their worker bees out in the open where the bees can be monitored more easily.

Bereft of partitions, we were squashed together in a smaller space to make room for the encroaching GINR members. There were no barriers now between me and the smokers, who were practically sitting in my lap. In a final blow, the light switch by my desk was sealed shut so that I wouldn't be able to turn off the fluorescent tubes over my head.

The nail that stuck up had been hammered down.

I was still documenting the evolving Ebisu enhancements, in the hope that my friend the Belgian semiconductor engineer would yet find a need for my well-chosen words. ("*Merci beaucoup, mademoiselle, votre Document de Release est très utile . . .*") I was still taking Japanese lessons from Mrs. Yamaguchi, and I had begun spending two hours a week with her husband, the chemistry professor, helping him with the scientific papers that he had to write in English. The only tricky part of these sessions occurred when Mr. Yamaguchi asked me questions like, "Rhiannon-*san*, what is the proper use of a present participle construction?"

I also took over Tessa's English classes for our colleagues. I gave three classes a week, one for beginners, one for intermediate students, and one for advanced students. I enjoyed the classes and so did the Tomodachi, as long as I watched my tendency to veer off on tangents. (In my advanced class, the Imp, having asked, intelligently, why the words "lung" and "pulmonary" don't look alike although they're related in meaning, got a half-hour lecture on the Latin, French, and Anglo-Saxon roots of the English language.)

For the beginners, bearing in mind my continuing bewilderment over particles, I concentrated on small but frequently-used words. We practiced saying, "*At* three o'clock *on* Wednesday *in* October." M.C. asked, "Rhiannon-*san*, why three words for saying same thing?" He got the same answer Mr. Yamaguchi got about present participle constructions. ("I don't know.")

The intermediate class struggled with idioms. "Why do you say, 'look it *up* in the dictionary?'" Teddy wanted to know. "The dictionary is not up, it is down here on the desk."

The advanced class included several SPN members who had made business trips to California, as well as others who hoped to, so I prepared lessons on making telephone calls and ordering food in restaurants. Passing out "menus" I'd typed up, I pretended to be a waitress, which sent the lads into fits of laughter.

"Soup or salad?" I asked.

"I'm sorry?" said Spats.

"You must choose, Kiyosawa-*san*. Soup or salad?"

"*Ah sō desu ka*! Soup *or* salad!" Turning to the others, Spats broke into excited Japanese. Enlightened looks dawned on several faces. "We have heard this in California," Spats said, turning back to me, "but we thought that the waitress was saying, 'Super salad.'"

Outside, as we sat studying English, it was almost always raining. "We're having good weather in Tokyo too," I wrote to Tessa, who had sent a heartless e-mail message from Healdsburg about blue sky and other distant memories. "If you were a reservoir, you'd be full. If you were a fish, you could swim down the street. But if you were a plastic frilled lizard of strange propensities and lurid coloring, you'd be pining for friends who have gone on to better, or at least drier, things."

Tessa had left Burt with me "to cheer you up." It was a kind thought, although cheered-up was not precisely how I felt when I walked into the office and saw Burt squatting on my terminal. My new cubicle-mate—that is, the man who would have been my cubicle-mate if we'd still had cubicles—did a much better job of raising my spirits. I hadn't known Ken Matsuda well before he came to Japan, but we became good friends. Without ever acting the least bit grumpy himself, he managed to convey that he found my grumpiness not only understandable but endearing. (Paul did not find my grumpiness endearing, which made sense, but had the effect of making me even grumpier.) Ken was full of praise for my technical writing, my progress with Japanese, and the good reports he heard from the lads about my English lessons. On my mental report card, the grades started inching up. Also, Ken was not a morning person. Sometimes I even reached the office ahead of my boss, instead of sidling in two hours after he'd started work.

The other Matsudas were equally congenial. Debby invited me to dinner frequently and accompanied me on outings, and

Rory moved into my heart next to Ikeda's daughter, Aya-*chan*.
"I love you, R'annon Matsuda!" he would cry, during one of
our joint baby-sitting sessions. He hadn't progressed far with
Hamlet's soliloquy; he was still stuck on "Not be!" Which, come
to think of it, would make a great slogan for a Japanese T-shirt.

Ikeda helped to cheer me up too. His cubicle—I could call
it that again, for new, short partitions had just gone up—was
next to Ken's and mine, and he began switching off the lights
for both cubicles at the master control panel. He wasn't concerned about premature aging of his skin, so it was obvious he
was doing this on my account. With both my bosses humoring
me, I finished the Ebisu Release Document with days to spare
and began working on the index. This proved so absorbing that
one Friday night I stayed at work till nine p.m. The lads—it
goes without saying that they were all still there—sent a del-
egation to my cubicle to ask if I was feeling all right.

Duncan had moved on to Benten, our new project. He sent
out a three-page memo full of issues and concerns; for example,
"Stack size can be reduced if needless variables in TDD000 are
removed and the TD-10 transaction file is converted from
KSAM to sequential." There was only one sentence I understood: "Beeping will be optional." I had to remind myself that I
hadn't understood Ebisu either, when I'd first read about it.

Christine had left HPJ to have her second child, a daughter,
Tomomi. Our new secretary, Miss Katsuki, a lovely and dignified young woman who was in my beginner's English class,
had already invited me to her wedding. Unlike Miyuki and
Christine, Miss Katsuki ("*kaht*-ski") asked to be called by her
last name, so we addressed her as Katsuki-*san*.

I had moved into hyper-save mode and my Fuji Bank account was flourishing. "By the end of May I'll be a yen mil-
lionaire," I wrote to Paul. "Thank you, thank you, thank you."

The cherry trees bloomed again in Tokyo. On a Wednesday
in mid-April—noted in my diary as "1st warm day!"—it stopped
raining long enough for our group's *o-hanami* (blossom-watch-

ing party). One of the freshmen camped all day under an especially fragrant tree in Inokashira Park to save a place for the
SPN group. Ken and I wondered why this was necessary until
we got there and found the park filled with people sitting on
plastic mats under the trees.

The blossom-watching party dates back to the Heian Era
(794–1192), when it was *the* social event of the season for members of the Imperial Court. Yoz had told me, in so many words,
that the point of *o-hanami* is to consider the cherry flowers as a
metaphor for the fleeting beauty of life. The *samurai* had been
especially fond of *sakura*, having spotted a similarity between
the short-lived blossoms and their own duty to die for their lords.

Japan's modern-day *samurai*, the salary-men, office ladies,
and families in Inokashira Park, were no doubt considering like
mad, but it was hard to tell because of all the eating, drinking,
and laughing that were going on. (The drinking has its down-
side. More than one hundred people die each year of alcohol
poisoning at *o-hanami*.)

After lubricating our vocal chords with beer, our group sang
several songs. Some of us didn't know the words and none of
us appeared to know the tunes, but we compensated with enthusiasm and a very high volume. The group next to us sang,
and then the group next to them sang. As the sky darkened and
the stars came out, a continuous chain of song wound through
the park. My colleagues consumed sea-creatures in enormous
quantities. Someone, probably Miyuki, had thoughtfully brought
a bucket of Kentucky Fried Chicken for poor tastebud-impaired
Rhiannon. What with the beer, the chicken, the laughter, and
the songs, it was like being back in college, except that every
once in a while, in the midst of a drink or a joke or a song, a
handful of cherry petals would drift down from the branches
and make me think about the fleeting beauty of life.

Twenty-Two

SEOUL SEARCHING

Early in May, I was asked to prepare some training materials and fly to Seoul for the purpose of explaining Ebisu (obsolete American software plus new Japanese enhancements) to South Koreans. This assignment made about as much sense as anything else I'd been asked to do, so I accepted.

I stayed with Gail Lowell, the Foreign Service Employee who had traveled with me in Hong Kong and China. South Korea was considered a hazardous posting, and Gail's benefits had been adjusted accordingly. She had a car and chauffeur, a two-story brick house with a front lawn, and a full-time housekeeper. It sounded like an enviable set-up until I found myself living in it. One of the housekeeper's duties was to wash Gail's fruit and vegetables in soapy water. Gail told me that I shouldn't even rinse my toothbrush under the tap lest I come down with what the English used to call "gyppy tummy." The chauffeur was polite, but South Korea is still recovering from an especially misogynist strain of Confucianism and I couldn't help feeling that he hated taking orders from a woman.

The engineers at Samsung Hewlett-Packard wanted to know what I thought of Seoul by comparison with Tokyo. It is no use asking me a question like this and expecting a worthwhile answer, because I suffer from an incurable need to tell people what I think they want to hear. I replied that I preferred Seoul because it has more open space, more trees, and fewer big buildings.

This got our sessions off to a good start, and the engineers went on being charming to me even as it emerged, over the course of two days, that they knew more about the Ebisu enhancements than I did. I took what consolation I could from the fact that it was my documentation, rushed to them several weeks before, that had brought them up to speed.

On Thursday, Gail and I flew to Cheju-do, an island off the southern coast of Korea, for a spot of vacation. When traveling, I normally sleep on trains or in one-star hotels with no elevator and a grubby bathroom down four flights of stairs, so our two nights on Cheju-do were a revelation. Our hotel had waterfalls in the lobby and a beach outside. A taxi (forty dollars for a full day's hire) drove us from scene to arresting scene: dry stone walls surrounding tangerine orchards, fields of bright gold flowers, burial mounds and prehistoric stone carvings, volcanic craters and old villages, and the longest known lava cave in the world.

Next day we hiked down the road to a cluster of turquoise-blue pools set in dark-gray rock. A nearby placard gave us to understand that these were no ordinary pools. In this place, it explained, "fairies came down from the heaven in the mid-night and took a bath at the three-step waterfall which spooted from the stiff."

This was hard to top, but Gail found a way. On my last evening in Seoul, she took me to a Swiss restaurant. Over a pot of bubbling cheese fondue, we toasted each other with California wine while a handsome South Korean waiter, engagingly turned out in a crisp white blouse and lederhosen, demonstrated his talent for yodeling.

The lads clustered around me when I returned to HPJ and asked what I thought of Seoul by comparison with Tokyo. I said I preferred Tokyo because it's modern and prosperous and has more big buildings.

"*Ah sō desu!*" The lads nodded with satisfaction.

Rumors are like earthquakes: they shake the ground under your feet. There had been lots of rumors during my stay in Japan: about the move to Hachioji, about the obsolescence, about hard times at home that might result in layoffs. The hard times turned out to be real, though temporary, and were handled with class. For several months, employees were given one Friday off per month and had their pay reduced by five percent (ten percent for managers). In return, no one got laid off. "Typical Bill and Dave," we e-mailed to each other, referring to HP's founders, Bill Hewlett and Dave Packard, who had always treated employees with consideration and respect.

While I'd been in South Korea, a new rumor had started making the rounds. "Management was considering options" that included disbanding our little group. John Young, then HP's president, had just visited Japan. SPN was supposed to be dead, he had reportedly said to HPJ's managers, so why was it lurching around Asia and Europe, biting companies on the neck and turning them into customers? "What do we have to do," he asked plaintively and in so many words, "dig up SPN's coffin and drive a stake through its heart?"

"It doesn't look good," Ken told me. But what about Benten, the Goddess of Love? "I wouldn't be in any hurry to start the documentation," Ken mused, gallantly ignoring the fact that he had never seen me in a hurry to do anything. There was a chance, he added, that HPJ might ask me to go home earlier than Christmas. How much earlier? Was, like, "tomorrow" a possibility? Ken didn't know. He didn't even know how soon *he* might be asked to go home, although his assignment was supposed to last for two years.

Things were going badly in Healdsburg too. Although Paul had worked for weeks on what Tessa called "the linguistics of keeping us all together," HP was shutting down the office. Tessa had been "surplussed," another new verb, but was still drawing a paycheck. The rest of Paul's employees were looking for work in other companies or HP divisions.

I was worried about Tessa, who kept sending me cryptic e-mail messages. I was also worried about Yoz, who was smoking more than ever and, I suspected, drinking more than ever too. After the company's annual physical—HPJ had its own doctor—Yoz was told to cut back, but he paid no attention. I was told that I had (1) anemia and (2) an infected tonsil. Second tests were performed that contradicted the findings of the first tests. Between the two rounds of tests, I broke out in hives. Was it possible, asked the HPJ doctor, touching the angry red bumps with a cautious finger, that I was going through a period of stress? "Please try not to worry," he advised me.

"HPJ management has decided to shove SPN back in the coffin and bury it," I wrote to Tessa on May 29. "No sales, not even in Japan, except some bells & whistles for Matsushita.* Samsung HP, having heard the news, has seized the dear departed and is trying to give it the kiss of life. They say we made a commitment, etc. I don't think it will get them anywhere, even with Gail flying here next week to kick up a fuss. I've been asked to stop working on Benten, which is easy because I haven't started, and devote the rest of my time to Ebisu training materials."

My departure date was eventually determined in typically Japanese fashion. Whenever I asked directly whether HPJ wanted me to leave sooner than January 1987, everyone got tongue-tied. I didn't want to outstay my welcome, so I gauged the extent of the remaining work and told Ken that I might want

---

* Matsushita Electric Company (MEC) was the customer that had requested the Ebisu enhancements.

to leave at the end of October. Ken told Ikeda; Ikeda told Ito-*san*; and Ito-*san* told the personnel department.

"Well, Nano," Ken said, a few days later, "I guess you'll be leaving at the end of October."

"*Ah sō desu,*" I said.

Twenty-Three

ALL EXISTENCE IS SUFFERING

Under the cellulitic sweeties at the Saffron restaurant, Ken, Yoz, Ikeda, and I helped Miyuki celebrate her twenty-fifth birthday. "I ate grotesque seafood," I reported to Tessa via e-mail, "and smoked—vicariously, thanks to Yoz—several cigarettes. It doesn't seem possible that a year has passed since my welcome-to-HPJ party at the Saffron restaurant. Time, as Ikeda puts it, flies like an arrow."

Cupid's arrows were flying too. On the first weekend in June, I attended two wedding receptions. At the reception for Dan Uno and his stunning young bride, Sumiyo, Yoz acted as master of ceremonies. In the days before, he bit his fingernails to the quick. "I must speak ex*tremely* polite Japanese," he fretted. "I must *not* make any mistakes, but this is so *diffi*cult!" I'd like to say he did a fine job, but of course I had no way of telling. He did catch the garter, by way of compensation. I hoped Miyuki would catch the bouquet, but she didn't.

The day before, Miyuki and I had met at Nishi Eifuku station and traveled on by train to the reception for Miss Katsuki, our new secretary. The reception was held in a hotel and fea-

tured a seven-course Western-style meal. I was the only Westerner present. I read a short speech that Miyuki had translated
into Japanese for me. Other guests made speeches. I could tell
they were using hyper-polite Japanese because they kept saying *"Watakushi"* instead of *"Watashi."** Several guests sang.
One of the songs, inevitably, was "I Just Called to Say I Love
You." Miss Katsuki—now Mrs. Ishizumi—started off in an orange kimono, elaborate black wig, and white make-up, and later
changed into a white wedding dress. She looked captivating in
both. I gave the bridal couple the wedding gift that is customary in Japan, money folded into a special envelope. (So much
more sensible than a toaster.) They gave me a lacquered basket.
Giving gifts to your wedding guests is also customary.

Back at the office, M.C., who'd taken over the systems-
guru role from Mr. Goodwrench, sent out a memo about our
computer, Himiko.

> How are you? I'm fine thank you, but Himiko-*chan* is not
> so. She has no more space to spool, because of shortage
> of disc space. We should purge our file and let Himiko-
> *chan* be fine. Why don't we hope Himiko-*chan* will have
> a good heart.

I printed out all my e-mail messages and then purged them
from the system. Himiko perked right up.

As head of marketing for the only part of SPN that was still
breathing, Ikeda had been asked to assume responsibility for
the relevant documentation. Thirteen manuals duly arrived on
tape from California, and Ikeda asked me to report on their condition. After several days of research, I was obliged to tell him
and Ken that the manuals reflected, with sad accuracy, SPN's
continuing indecision with regard to word-processing tools.
They had been written in three different word processors.

---

* Have you forgotten already? *Watashi* means "I."

"I don't believe it," Ken said.

Ikeda said something in Japanese that did not sound polite at all.

"Can we convert them all to CML?" Ken asked. CML was our current word processor.

"Most of them."

"So . . . how long will this conversion take, Rhiannon-*san*?"

"At least seven months."

"Seven months!" said Ikeda. He looked faint.

I felt like kicking someone. Ikeda had recently procured a modem for me, driven me home with it, and hooked it up to Bunter so I could dial in to Himiko and work at home a few days a week, out of the cigarette smoke. I could only imagine what battles he'd had to fight with higher management on my behalf. (Not that he gave any hint of having fought battles. He acted as if he'd never had more fun in his life.) Kenichi Ikeda was the last person at HPJ to whom I wanted to give bad news.

Worse news came that afternoon. CML had not yet been designated as an official Hewlett-Packard product, so we couldn't send documentation in CML on tape to outside customers. "We're converting everything in CML back into older word processors," wrote my colleague from California. "You'll have to do the same."

Reluctantly, with Ken standing beside me for moral support, I gave this message to my Japanese boss. "*Ah sō desu ka*," Ikeda said calmly. In the hours that had passed since my first report, he had remembered that, as a Japanese native, he was part of the great Buddhist tradition. All existence is suffering. The cause of this suffering is selfish desire. We should cultivate serenity and not be too attached to the things of this world. We must learn to let go of our wish, however commendable it might seem to us, to be able to revise, print, and mail the SPN manuals to our customers in a speedy and efficient manner.

I stood sadly in Ikeda's cubicle, thinking of all the projects I'd learned to let go of over the years. My Master Glossary of

SPN Terms, for example, which would have helped the Belgian semiconductor engineer (*"Mais formidable!"*) as well as encouraged SPN writers to use the same words for the same things. I'd started it when I joined Hewlett-Packard in 1982. It was half-finished when I acquired a new boss, who told me that there wasn't going to be time in our schedule for the Master Glossary of SPN Terms.

One must kill one's desires in order to be released from suffering.

Ikeda cleared his throat and spoke. There was a little something I could do for HPJ, he intimated, if it wouldn't interfere too much with my halting progress toward Nirvana.

"Of course, Ikeda-*san*. Just tell me what it is."

"So . . . Duncan-*san* and I have been talking, and we would like to ask you to write a Master Glossary of SPN Terms."

One Monday afternoon a few weeks later, I sat alone in my cubicle, working on the Master Glossary. The exercise music was playing, and as usual the lads were ignoring it. Someone had brought in a bag of cherries, the first of the season, and the lads had gathered around Okada's desk to share them. The atmosphere was jollier than usual because all the managers were away. Okada was at Matsushita, Ito-*san* and Ikeda were meeting off-site, and Ken had taken a day of vacation to recover from the party that he and Debby had given on Saturday.

It had been a great party. Mrs. Ishizumi had brought her new husband. Easy Rider had brought his new motorcycle. ("I am not a *bōsōzoku* boy," he assured me solemnly.) Yoz had drunk too much. Everyone had stayed until eleven-thirty and helped clean up, toting dishes to the kitchen, running the garbage disposal, trying to figure out how the dishwasher worked, etc.

I'd enjoyed the party. In fact, I'd been happy for several days. In another attempt to cut costs, HP had come up with a new program for divisions that were currently short of work. It was called VTO (Voluntary Time Off). Nothing could have struck a more responsive chord in me, unless it was a program called VTOPFB (Voluntary Time Off Plus Free Books). By the time I got home I'd be reduced to a whimpering ruin, bowing at random, laughing hysterically whenever I saw a user manual, apologizing to everyone for being so tall. It would be best for all concerned if HP tucked me quietly out of sight until I recovered.

Corporate headquarters had written to ask if I'd be interested in VTO. I had written back that "interested" was not the word. "Passionately enthusiastic" was a better description of my attitude. I noted further that my division was not just short of work, it was dead and buried. That should clinch it, I'd thought. Now, what would I do with my time off? Finish *Terminal Death* . . . visit my friends in England . . . learn how to cook properly . . . and I could finally get around to reading Dostoevski.

Laughter flowed over the short cubicle walls from Okada's desk. I sat glaring at my terminal, which was displaying an e-mail message from Corporate. My division had just been resurrected under a new name and had so much work to do that someone would meet me at the airport to start briefing me. Sorry, Rhiannon. No VTO.

I tried to be calm, like Ikeda. I tried to cultivate serenity. I tried to learn to let go.

I picked up Burt and flung him at the wall.

People at Hewlett-Packard were being given Voluntary Time Off and I wasn't going to be one of them. I grabbed my handbag and stalked out of the building. It couldn't get any worse than this.

A hand fell on my shoulder. Hot lips slobbered against my neck. A voice whispered hoarsely in my ear. "Hey, baby. Remember me?"

Thag was back.

Twenty-Four

IMPRESSING THE THOMPSONS

The Thompsons and I sat in the Bullet Train. Outside, scenery was blurring past at 130 miles per hour, but since most of it looked like Tokyo I didn't care how fast it went. The Thompsons were reading what our friend Clare Manifold calls "worthy and improving literature." I was brooding over the shadow that, as T.S. Eliot says, falls between the Idea and the Reality.

I had invited all my friends to visit me in Tokyo. I didn't know where I'd be living after I left Japan, so it seemed wise to solicit guests while I still had a room to put them in. The Thompsons were the only people who rose to my bait, planning a visit for ten days in September. Ann is English and John is Canadian. He sounds English, though. For example, he refers to himself as "one," something that Americans never do because it would cut down on the number of times we can fit "I" into a sentence. John, on the other hand, says things like, "Would one be correct in assuming that one ought to come prepared for inclement weather?"

John and Ann are academics. Whenever I hear from them, they're simultaneously proofreading the galleys of their latest

199

books* and getting ready to pop over to Berlin or Florence or Washington, D.C. to give a paper or do research or take up a prestigious fellowship. You'd think they'd have the decency to be absent-minded professors, but in fact they're so well-organized that everywhere they go, they find the best restaurants, trendiest galleries, most interesting museums. And they've read *everything*.

In short, the Thompsons are what I longed to be, Sophisticated World Travelers. They're also superb cooks. I had stayed with them many times and seen them wander casually into the kitchen and wander out again an hour later with a perfectly cooked duck à l'orange under one arm. A meal *chez* Thompson is a meal to be remembered, whereas I've given dinner parties after which my guests had to stop at Burger King on their way home because they were still hungry.

So although I was pleased that John and Ann were coming, I was also intimidated. But after all, I reassured myself, I was no longer the Rhiannon Paine they'd met in Liverpool in 1978, an impoverished M.A. student analyzing the poems of Thomas Hardy in a studio flat with no phone and indifferent heating. I'd come a long way, baby.

Besides, this was the Thompsons' first visit to Japan. They'd be cowed, poor things, by the noise, the crowds, the traffic, the language, and by Thag, who was still skulking about. My friends would rely on me, the local resident, to lead them around, interpret for them, answer their questions, find them the nearest place with Western food and air-conditioning. For once, I'd be the one who was clued-in.

The Thompsons had arrived and immediately started asking questions. What had the impact of Confucianism been on the established Shinto and Buddhist religions? Had the Impe-

---

* Ann's first book, *Shakespeare's Chaucer: A Study in Literary Origins*, was available for purchase on the sixth floor at Kinokuniya, and she and John had just finished a joint book on metaphor.

rial Court been in Nara or Kyoto in the time of Murasaki Shikibu? Which was the best museum for *netsuke*? (*Netsuke*? What the hell was *netsuke*?) I'd been hoping for questions I could answer. "Where can we buy Shredded Wheat?" for example, or something about Shop Floor Control.

Thag had thrown his weight around but he didn't faze my friends. "A bit of warm weather is refreshing, actually." After several days of that, Thag had slunk away, defeated. The noise, the crowds, and the traffic didn't bother John and Ann at all. "Oh, were there dogs barking last night?" They went to both Kabuki and Noh, which was more than I ever did. On their second day in Tokyo, they set off contentedly, without me, to take the Inokashira Line to the Suntory Museum. On their way back they popped into the Summit supermarket and bought some seafood. (I never bought seafood in Tokyo. I couldn't get past the packages of octopus.) Then they came home and cooked dinner for me. It was delicious.

The Bullet Train flew southwest. Ann turned a page in her worthy and improving book. John had fallen asleep, but he was probably dreaming about some fascinating aspect of post-structuralist cinematic theory. In French.

I closed my eyes. I saw myself the week before, standing with the Thompsons in a travel agency—not the one in Kichijoji; a different agency, where the staff was supposed to understand more English. I had undertaken a series of bilingual dialogues, supplemented with mime, that resulted two hours later in the train and hotel reservations for our present journey. The cost was one hundred ninety thousand yen, around fourteen hundred dollars. I saw the three of us going through our wallets and coming up with about half that amount in cash. I heard myself saying to the Thompsons, "We'll go withdraw the rest of the money from my Fuji Bank account. We can work out who-owes-what later."

The scene shifted to a Fuji Bank several blocks away. Here, I was thinking, was an opportunity to impress the Thompsons

with my mastery of the Japanese Automated Teller Machine—
a mastery based on a yellow Post-It note stuck in the back of
my address book. (Japanese ATM's are of course labeled entirely in Japanese.) The instructions on the Post-It note read as
follows:

1. Press far left button.
2. Insert card.
3. Magic # (keyboard).
4. Amount.
5. Denomination.
6. Yen symbol.
7. Confirm (button between 0 and X).

I had long since memorized which buttons to push. As the
Thompsons looked on, full of academic interest, I attacked the
ATM with confidence. "Let's see, we need about eighty-thou-
sand yen . . . I'll withdraw one hundred thousand."* I pressed,
inserted, typed. The machine disgorged a fat wad of money in
ten-thousand-yen notes. I looked at it dubiously. It was a very
fat wad, as fat as one of those Dostoevski novels I'd planned to
read during my Voluntary Time Off. Should I count it? Thag
was still with us, so I was *mushi-atsui* (hot and humid) as well
as exhausted from trying to sound impressive in scraps of un-
grammatical Japanese.

"Okay. Let's go back and pay," I said.

Scene shift. Travel agency. Flanked by John and Ann, I handed the wad of money to our agent. "*Jū man-en desu* (one hundred thousand yen)," I said.

The young woman's eyes widened. As her right hand accepted the yen notes, her left hand flew up to cover her mouth.
She could have been a statue labeled, "Speak no evil but carry

---

* You can withdraw as much money as you like from an ATM in
Japan, up to the total amount in your bank account.

a big wad of money." Quickly she mastered herself. Turning away to shield the notes from other agents and customers, she counted it with swift slim fingers. Then she turned back to me. "*Iie, chigai masu* (No, that is not correct)," she said softly. "*Hyaku man-en desu.*"

It was barely a whisper, but heads turned all over the room. Eyes looked at me and then slid away as I stood there, sweating with embarrassment, working it out. *Hyaku man* . . . one hundred times ten thousand . . . that was (I fought the urge to whip out my calculator) . . . that was one million. I had given the young woman one million yen—about seven thousand dollars. I'd pressed an extra zero on the Automatic Teller Machine.

Scene shift. Several days later. The Thompsons and I were en route to Hakone. We'd been traveling for about an hour when Ann began to evince signs of distress. The train, it seemed to her, was not going in the right direction. She suggested that I ask someone where we were headed. I demurred. I knew that we had boarded the train for Hakone, and trains don't suddenly jump off their tracks and veer off across country to alternative destinations. I was surprised that I should have to point this out to Ann, who lives in a place where you can still travel everywhere by rail.

Ann wasn't reassured. As the train chugged on, she became increasingly convinced that something was amiss. Finally, swallowing large indigestible chunks of pride, I turned to a fellow passenger. "*Sumimasen . . . kono densha wa, Hakone ni ikimasu ka?*" It was mortifying to have to ask, but at least I remembered to say "train" instead of "telephone."

"*Iie, chigai masu,*" replied the passenger. "*Kamakura ni ikimasu.*"

How do you say "Oh shit" in Japanese?

I toyed with the idea of carrying on to Kamakura and telling the Thompsons that it was Hakone, but I knew it wouldn't work. It would have worked with me all right, but the Thompsons had undoubtedly read up on both places and would spot the substitution.

So I had to confess. "I don't know how, but we got on the wrong train," I said. "This is the train to Kamakura."

Our fellow passenger intervened. Using a few words of English and a set of ingenious hand signals, he explained that we had boarded the correct train; however, at an earlier station, the train had divided itself in two, like a worm reproducing, and the two parts had taken off in different directions. It was the part of the train we *weren't* on that was headed for Hakone.

Impossible to avoid the conclusion that one's friends were not impressed with one's mastery of life in Tokyo, despite the fact that one had recently performed prodigies of cross-cultural communication. Perhaps, I thought, gazing out at the fuzzy scenery, I should stop trying to impress the Thompsons and just enjoy their company.

Ann closed her book; John sighed and woke up; and the Bullet Train pulled into Kurashiki.

Twenty-Five

MUSEUMS AND MAPLE-LEAVES

Kurashiki (usually pronounced "koor-*ahsh*-key") means "warehouse village," a name that's about as romantic as a boiled eel. Apt, too, you think, as you emerge from the train station. But walk for ten minutes and you enter another world. The old town center is full of whitewashed plaster buildings trimmed with tiles in lattice patterns of black, gray, and brown, and topped with black-tiled roofs. On the River Kurashiki—a ribbon of green water that used to carry barges loaded with rice—swans glide under arched stone bridges between feathery willow trees.

The town was a small village at the beginning of the seventeenth century. When the Shogunate established an administrative office there, Kurashiki became a marketing center for sake, cotton, and rice. The beautiful old warehouses that used to store these commodities are now private residences, museums, and inns.

A friend had recommended the Ryokan Kurashiki, a set of converted rice and sugar warehouses unified with wood-beamed ceilings, wood and tatami-mat floors, polished antique furniture, *shōji* screens, and a mossy green garden. The staff were accustomed to foreigners and correctly interpreted my halting explanation that, whereas John and Ann did not mind taking a hot bath together, neither of them was interested in bathing with me or anyone else. "*Hitori de,*" I said, pointing to myself. "Alone." The staff looked sympathetic. ("Poor thing . . . rejected for bathing by her English friends . . . let us treat her with special care.")

I loved the staff, the *ryokan*, and old-town Kurashiki. Buildings, right here in Japan, that weren't shrines or temples but weren't ugly! In the morning I plunged about taking photographs of roofs and walls until John and Ann grabbed an arm each and steered me to the Ohara Art Gallery. There I fell into further ecstasies, for the building is modeled on a Greek temple. Western architecture, right here in Japan! What's that? Okay, mid-Eastern architecture! I plied my camera until the Thompsons suggested, with that force and clarity which typifies the academic mind, that the main point of art galleries is to go inside them and look at art.

Emerging several hours later, drunk on El Greco and Picasso and Rodin, we ate a quick lunch and then started through the Museum of Folk Craft. Folk art is a favorite of mine, partly because it's the only kind of art I can imagine myself creating, and I wandered happily through the four converted rice-stores. Luminous glass bottles in turquoise, violet, sea-green . . . paper dyed in rainbow colors . . . mats woven with diamond, arrowhead, and checkerboard designs . . . shapely pottery and baskets . . . furniture in which every grain and whorl of wood served the design . . . finely woven textiles striped like a plowed field, or dark wavy green like wind blowing over the tops of pine trees, or white dappled on blue like the ocean on a rough day. Amazing to think that ordinary people created these things and that other ordinary people got to use them.

Next day we traveled south again and took the ferry to Miyajima, "shrine island," whose real name is Itsukushima. You've seen pictures of it; it's the place where the orange-gold *torii* stands in the sea—the largest *torii* in Japan, its pillars fifty-three feet high, its lintel seventy-six feet long. As our ferry sailed across Hiroshima Bay toward the island, mist was lifting from every hill and mountain, as if the land were evaporating and turning back to air. It looked magical. "Be not afeard: the isle is full of noises . . ."

Until the Meiji Restoration, says Baedeker's, Miyajima was a sacred island on which no one could either be born or die. Picture a raging storm, a typhoon, a tempest, lashing the island, forcing the trees to bow as rain pours from the screaming skies. A knot of men come hurrying toward the shore, carrying a terrified young woman in the throes of sudden labor, or an old man who isn't expected to last the night. Shouting over the storm, they set the outcast into a boat and push it out to sea. Did some courageous volunteer try to sail the boat across to safety? Or was the helpless passenger sent off to give birth or die alone?

There is still no cemetery on Miyajima. Islanders who take their dead to the mainland for burial must perform rites of purification before they can return. Dogs are banned to protect the tame fallow deer that walk beside you through the streets, like the fawn that accompanies Alice through the nameless wood in Looking-Glass Land. Pull out a sandwich or a package of potato chips, though, and the deer reveal their true character. They are moochers. "Hey man, got any bread?" These are Eurasian deer (*Dama dama* or *Dama mesopotamica*). They have yellowish coats, spotted with white in summer.

We took a funicular railway up Mount Misen—one mile, fifty minutes, 1739 feet—to the island's highest point, and were rewarded with an astonishing view of the Inland Sea as a sheet of silver, set with dark little islands that look as if they haven't changed since they dripped off the *kami*'s spear at the beginning of time.

"Shall we walk back down?" John asked.

"Walk?" I temporized.

"Otherwise one would feel that one hadn't truly experienced the mountain."

The only thing I wanted to experience was a hot meal, but Ann was equally keen on the walking concept. I am an orange-juice-injected Californian who spent her formative years breathing fresh air under palm trees, whereas the Thompsons are England-dwelling professors who spend most of their time reading. Guess which of us bounded down the mountain like fallow deer and which of us went staggering after, slipping on rocks and banging her head into tree branches? I can truthfully say that Mount Misen was experienced by virtually every square inch of my body. My bottom, for example, came into contact with the mountain on several occasions, and experienced it as hard. Also rocky.

We reached sea level eventually and toured the Itsukushima Shrine. Founded in 593,* the shrine is dedicated to three princesses, daughters of our old friend Susano-wo, the Impetuous Male, who is also the moon, sea, and storm god. There's no point in looking for fourteen-hundred-year-old buildings, though. Shrines and temples are made primarily of wood, so they are frequently rebuilt. The present structure consists of a Main Shrine and several other buildings—Offerings Hall, House of Prayer, Purification Hall—all joined by covered walkways. They stand on pilings sunk into the bay, a series of white walls framed in red-and-gold-painted timber, enchanting even when the water is low. When the tide comes in, the pilings disappear, the gray-green roofs merge with the pine-covered hills, and the shrine looks as if it's sailing onto the island.

On our last morning on Miyajima, while the Thompsons finished packing, I went out into the chilled mid-September air to buy a souvenir. In an old-fashioned shop, long and low, lit

---

* According to the Japan National Tourist Organization. Baedeker's says that it's first mentioned in 811.

with lamps, I found some small, inexpensive pâpier-maché trays that had red maple leaves pressed into them, like the leaves that were scattered on the ground outside the shop. While I waited for the trays to be wrapped—nothing is ever just stuck into a paper bag in Japan—I sank heavily onto a wooden bench and closed my eyes. I hadn't slept well the night before, my legs and back ached, and my knees were trembling after yesterday's hike down Mount Misen. (Komori, one of the freshmen, told me that in Japan this phenomenon is known as "laughing knees.")

Someone spoke to me. One of the women from the shop was standing beside the bench, holding my parcel. I started to rise, but she put her hand on my arm. "*Osuwari-ni natte kudasai* (please sit)," she said in very polite Japanese. Another woman walked up and handed me a round cup of green tea and a warm, fragrant, doughy cookie. Both women smiled and bowed. Then they left me to sip and eat in peace.

I watched them serve other customers and saw that this wasn't part of the shop's standard service. It was a spontaneous act, rare in Japan where there are rules for everything and you have to worry about saddling people with obligations they can't repay. The women had recognized that I was cold and tired. They had seen me looking at my watch, biting my lip, picking nervously at my hair. They wanted me to take the time to rest and look through the open door at the view outside, and it's because of them that I can still see the sun shining on the red maple trees of Miyajima.

A cup of tea and sympathy
A last gift from
The magic island

Twenty-Six

NOT PORTABLE PEOPLE

"*Nihon ni kita toki wa, nihonjin no tomodachi wa zenzen arimasen deshita.*" I paused to take a breath. Mrs. Yamaguchi smiled encouragingly. I was reading her the farewell speech I'd written for the Tomodachi. Translated, it read:

"When I came to Japan, I had no Japanese friends. Now I am happy because I have so many wonderful friends like you. Not only have you worked very hard with computers, but you have also improved your speaking of English. Thanks to everyone here, I have enjoyed my time in Japan very much. I will never forget you. Please come to California soon."

I looked up from my paper. Tears were running down Mrs. Yamaguchi's face.

"*Sumimasen!*" I said. "I'm sorry. Does my speech contain a rudeness?"

"Oh, no, Rhiannon-*san*," said my teacher, wiping her eyes. "I am crying because I am happy that you have learned such good Japanese."

I sat there preening myself for several minutes . . . as long as it took Mrs. Yamaguchi to find a handkerchief, pat her cheeks dry, and wipe her glasses. Maybe I hadn't done so badly at this *nihongo* stuff! After all, I had written a speech—quite a number of sentences, actually, and using some rather advanced syntax—in perfect Japanese.

Mrs. Yamaguchi put her handkerchief away, picked up a pencil, and reached for the paper. "I will just mark a few corrections, Rhiannon-*san*."

After a last week of rainy, metal-gray days, the rain dried up and the sun came out. I turned off my air conditioner, opened my windows, and started trying to appreciate everything. It was the end of September. I had one month left in Japan.

I was still working on *Terminal Death*. "I've just added a new character," I reported to Tessa, "which means rewriting the first half for the fourth time." I had begun to despair of ever finishing my novel, let alone getting it published.

What did get published was the Ebisu Release Document. It's called *The SPN System Enhancements from HPJ (Phase 1.5)*. It has a pale-turquoise cover. It contains 327 carefully-written pages and a 14-page index, plus graphics that illustrate the new station/operation relationship, Stream 6 data collection, a sample diffusion aisle, etc. I don't know if anyone ever read it. I never heard from the Belgian semiconductor engineer.

I finished the Master Glossary and gave it to Ikeda. As my last project, he asked me to revise the SPN online help system.

My Fuji Bank balance was still rising. By mid-October I had almost twenty-five thousand dollars, six times as much as I'd ever had before. Paul had told me that I would get a suitcase stuffed with money, and Paul had told me the truth.

"It's too much," I said to Ken, one day at the office. "What am I going to do with it?"

Ken looked intrigued. He wasn't familiar with the concept of "too much money."

"I thought I'd save maybe ten thousand," I explained. "And then I could go live somewhere cheap, Liverpool maybe, and

NOT PORTABLE PEOPLE ✺ 213

make the money last for a year while I wrote another novel. But I haven't finished *this* novel yet, and now I've got all this extra money. I mean, it seems like I should do something mature and responsible with it."

Ken agreed that it did.

"But what? You've tried to explain the difference between stocks and bonds, but I still don't get it. And I'm not sure I agree with the stock market. It's basically just gambling, isn't it? Bingo for the rich?"

Ken allowed that there was an element of chance involved. Investment, on the other hand, allowed companies to develop their potential.

"Yes, but *which* companies? I wouldn't want to invest in companies that make cigarettes or napalm or, like, really bad software. Anyway, you have to know what you're doing, don't you?"

Ken nodded. You certainly did.

"And I don't."

This was indisputable.

"Real estate," Ken said.

"Real estate," I repeated, blankly.

"You should buy a house."

Ken is the type of person who hides his light under a bushel, whereas I am the type of person who waves her light about and points to it. Thus it had taken me a while to figure out how intelligent he is. But I'd been sharing a cubicle with him for six months and for much of that time we'd been underworked, so I'd got to know him pretty well. I knew that he'd earned a degree in biochemistry, as well as his MBA, from U.C. Berkeley. I'd gathered that he was seriously smart about money. So when Ken told me that I should buy a house, I thought about it for approximately thirty seconds and then I said, "Okay."

As if on cue, Miyuki appeared in our cubicle to ask if I'd like to buy the furniture in my apartment from HPJ. The company would give me a sixty percent discount, she said, because the furniture was used.

"But I'm the one who used it!" I pointed out. "So it hardly seems fair for me to get a discount—"

"Rhiannon," Ken said. "Buy the furniture."

So I bought the furniture, including the green curtains from Fabrications and the off-white curtains with their pattern of transparent leaves, which turned out to be the most expensive item. The fabric had been imported from Belgium, Miyuki told me, and had cost almost a thousand dollars.

A team of movers came to the House of Clear Water to estimate the weight of my possessions. Bunter the computer, books, stereo, curtains, rugs, stripped-pine whatnots, a dozen shoeboxes full of photographs, my copy of *The SPN System Enhancements from HPJ (Phase 1.5)*, and one plastic frilled lizard . . . about 2500 pounds, the movers reckoned.

I finished revising the SPN online help system. "Congratulations for your honest effort for this item," Ikeda wrote to me. "Your effort will help us so greatly."

And then there was nothing left to do but go to parties. Debby and I gave a shower for Duncan's wife, Linette, who was expecting their first child. She was going to have the baby in Japan, which I considered brave of her, but then I think it's brave to have a baby anywhere.

Mrs. Yamaguchi gave a kimono party at her house for Debby and me. Putting on a kimono turns out to be a complicated procedure, like the new station/operation relationship but involving a number of mysterious undergarments. The process takes about forty minutes and we felt limp by the time we were dressed, but it didn't matter. Once you've got a kimono on, vigorous activity is pretty much out of the question. The sash around the ribs that looks so fetching on a Japanese woman takes an hourglass figure like mine and punishes it for every hamburger it's ever eaten.

Debby's kimono was pale blue and mine was camellia-pink. We look pretty in the pictures that Mrs. Yamaguchi took, as long as you ignore our stubbornly Western heads.

Ken and I invited my English students, soon to be his English students, to dinner at a new restaurant in Kichijoji. "I heard Zap's is a very exciting place," wrote Spats in his acceptance message. Komori wrote that he would attend "with pleasure." Teddy accepted too, though he warned he'd have to "quickly eat and drink, because Kichijoji is just so far to my house." Easy Rider couldn't come—he was taking the day off to ride his motorcycle to Nozawa—but he asked us to "please enjoy special party."

"I hope this party will be one of your Japanese memories," the Imp wrote. I don't remember the party at all. I was tired already and there were several parties left to go.

I was still worried about Tessa—the cryptic e-mail messages kept coming—and about Yoz. HPJ was planning a reorganization and Yoz had been assigned to another group. I didn't understand the implications, but I could tell from his e-mail messages that he wasn't happy.

> In the politics, I was suspended in the new organization
> . . . This morning, I was asked whether I'd like to accept
> this job. I could not find any reason to deny, so that this
> new assignment would be effective . . . Maybe you'll say
> it's interesting, but I don't think so. But I'm an employee
> . . . so that I cannot deny. It's so sad but true in Japan.

I took Yoz to dinner at a French restaurant. As we sipped our wine, I asked him if he wouldn't be happier living in the U.S. He'd been there several times on business trips so he knew what he'd be getting into. I was sure that California would be a more comfortable environment than Japan for a fellow misfit.

Yoz lit a cigarette, inhaled, and turned to blow the smoke away from me. "California is *great*," he said, turning back. "But

I get homesick for the *history* and *traditions*, the familiar *food*, and for speaking Japanese with *other* people. For me, English is very interesting and *fun*. But it can't say what I *want* to say."

For two and a half years, Yoz had hung out with Americans. He had climbed over the wall to meet us on our side. He had learned our slang and called us by nicknames. But he'd tried to help me over the wall to his side, too. He had told me more about his country than anyone else. He was the only one of my Japanese friends who ever grumbled, who ever said anything negative, who ever sounded like me. He had let me see the cost of being Japanese—but then he had shown me an ancient dance and a magic gorge as if to tell me: *It is worth it.*

I had misjudged him. He wasn't a portable person any more than I was. He was going back to his side of the wall.

I hate walls. I suppose they're necessary, but I hate them anyway.

"You'll visit me in California," I said. "And we'll write to each other."

"*Hai, sō desu!*" said Nakamura-*san*.

"Rhiannon-*san* . . ." Miyuki said, later that week. We were standing on the train from Shibuya, homeward-bound after attending a meeting of Miyuki's English Conversation Club.

"Yes, Miyuki-*san*?"

"I have done a terrible thing."

When some people tell you they've done a terrible thing, you start edging away from them, envisioning a bank in flames or the bodies of disemboweled animals. With other people, and this is the category I fall into, you assume some lesser sin, such as forgetting a best friend's birthday or declaring the spare bathroom as a business office. (*Jōdan deshita*, Internal Revenue Service! The room I declare doesn't have any plumbing.)

There is a third category of people who when they say "I've done a terrible thing" cause you to goggle at them unattractively because you can't, no matter how hard you try, imagine them doing anything wrong. I stood there hanging onto my strap and tried to think what terrible thing Miyuki could have done. My best effort was, *She accidentally took a pen home from the office and then, before she could return it, she lost it.*

"Would you like to tell me about it?" I asked.

"I will get off at Nishi Eifuku," Miyuki said.

She wouldn't walk home with me, although I urged her to, so we sat on a bench in Nishi Eifuku station. As trains clattered in and out, Miyuki told me about the terrible thing she had done.

She had accepted a job with IBM.

"A good job?" I asked, puzzled.

"Oh yes, Rhiannon-*san*. They have asked me to be an International Assignments Representative. I will help people who come from different countries to work in Japan. I think it is a big promotion from my work for HPJ."

"And will you earn more money?"

"About twenty-five percent more."

"But Miyuki-*san*, that's wonderful!"

Miyuki shook her head. Tears were running down her face. "No, it is terrible. I am being disloyal to Ikeda-*san* and all my friends at HPJ."

My head was crammed full of useful information about Japan, which is a small mountainous country with few natural resources. I knew all about *dantai*, the group that offers security in exchange for loyalty, and the Table of Obligations and their Reciprocals. I knew that the entire class gets punished when one child disobeys, and that if you buy a Japanese person a gift, however ill-considered and insignificant, and offer it by saying *tsumaranai mono desu ga*, "It's just a little thing," which you must say even if you're giving someone a yacht full of diamonds, you will get a gift in return. I knew about the attachment to hierarchy and the desire of each person to find her proper place. Everything I'd read, committed to memory, and thought I understood about Japan suddenly condensed itself and turned into flesh, in the person of this friend sitting beside me. This was what it all meant. When you got a better job, you cried over your own treachery.

As Tessa might have said, I was "dumbfounded." I sat there speechless, with my culture's ground-rules breaking apart around me. What about the imperative to Go For It? What about Looking After Number One? Promotions are good! More money is excellent! This was splendid news, it was a triumph! Wasn't it?

A train pulled into the station, bound for Kichijoji. The doors clanged open and people got off. They glanced with quickly-concealed curiosity at Miyuki, who had buried her face in her hands, and at the worried-looking *gaijin* sitting beside her. I thought I could tell what they were thinking. *Ah sō desu. This is what happens when you consort with foreigners. It will always end in tears.*

Miyuki had helped me furnish my apartment. She had translated my speeches, set up my Fuji Bank account, and taken me to concerts. When I got a bad case of flu before Christmas, she had taken an afternoon off work to bring me groceries. I hadn't asked her, she'd just called up and said she was on her way over, what did I need? She had never asked for anything in return. And now, for the first time, she needed my help.

I'm a firstborn, an older sister, and I have a wide streak of protective instinct. If I could have saved Miyuki's life by throwing myself in front of the next train, I would have done it instantly. I'm not saying I'd do this for just anyone, you understand. In fact there are some people I'd just as soon push under the train. I would have done it for Miyuki, though. But the situation didn't warrant a melodramatic and final gesture. All Miyuki needed was advice and encouragement. But I didn't know what to say.

I took refuge in facts. "Will you turn down the job?" I asked.

Miyuki shook her head. It might hurt her to leave Hewlett-Packard Japan, but she was going to do it anyway.

I told her what I hoped was true, that Ikeda and our other colleagues liked her so much they'd be happy for her. "You're a pioneer," I added.

Miyuki sat up straight, pulled out a handkerchief, and started drying her eyes. "A pioneer?" she asked doubtfully. I think she was picturing herself in a calico dress on the bench of a covered wagon.

"You're doing something different. You're setting off into new territory. It's always hard to be a pioneer, Miyuki-*san*, but it will be worth it. I think you're very brave."

For a long time afterward, I believed I let Miyuki down that day. It has taken me years and lots more reading to understand that Japanese reserve is not, fundamentally, about pride. It isn't a means of establishing a one-up position over a person who can't hide her emotions. Nor is it only about *giri*-to-one's-name. It is rooted in consideration for the feelings of others. The Japanese see it like this: when you display grief or anger, you cause distress and anxiety to the people around you, which you have no right to do. Your loved ones especially must be protected, so you can't break down even at home or with close friends. "Smile, though your heart is breaking," is the general idea.

But Miyuki knew that I wouldn't think her display of emotion was rude. She knew that I probably hadn't a clue (and I didn't, then) that rudeness was even an issue. I wasn't Japanese, so I wouldn't think, "Miyuki's crying and making me feel bad, how dare she!" She understood my culture. She understood me. What helped her wasn't my clumsy words, but the mere fact of my being there, a foreigner, someone she could talk to. Miyuki didn't confide in me because of what I knew and could tell her by way of advice. She confided in me because of what I didn't know.

The God of Irony was hovering over the bench that afternoon.

In the days that followed, Miyuki needed all her pioneer's courage. To my great relief, Ito-*san* and Ikeda *were* happy for her. "They are so nice," she wrote in an e-mail message to me, "and want me to come back if I have any problem there." But she had two months to work for HPJ after giving her notice, and company policy dictated that she couldn't tell anyone else why she was going. An American could have joked about it— "Wait and see. You won't believe it!"—but we're raised to believe that we can plug ourselves painlessly into and out of groups. Most Japanese can't. It's not a question of pulling a plug, but of severing cords that grow out of each person in the group and connect her to the others. The knife, cutting the cords, seems to cut into living flesh.

That's the metaphor I used as I tried to understand Miyuki's anguish. I found her one day crying quietly in the ladies' room. After trying to console her, ineffectually again, I sent her an e-mail message. She replied, "Yesterday I felt sad when I talked with a sales manager in Osaka whom I have known since I joined HPJ. He does not know that I am leaving." And then she changed the subject. "Rhiannon-*san*, please enjoy yourself in Japan this month."

I didn't try to persuade Miyuki that she'd be better off living in California. She wasn't a portable person either.

Twenty-Seven

THE HEART OF JAPAN

During my final weeks in Japan I felt alert and exhausted at the same time, charged with nervous energy but too tired to move. "I just want to get out of here," I wrote to Tessa, "so I can settle down in California and *write*. But I'm afraid I'll die before I get home, leaving *Terminal Death* unfinished and all this dues-paying for nought."

I could see the gods—a mixed bag from the Japanese pantheon and the Greek and Roman deities, who were always knocking up nymphs and turning people into trees—rubbing their hands and saying, "She's worked for eighteen months, she's saved a lot of money . . . let's make sure that she never gets to enjoy it." How would they kill me? Plane crash? Tainted rice? Errant taxi driver?

American Run Down on the Inokashira Dōri
Unfinished Novel Found in Backpack,
Stained with Häagen-Dazs

I sat down at my computer and wrote a will. I never printed it or told anyone it was there. It wasn't intended as a will. It was a challenge to the gods: "Now that you know I'm prepared to die, you won't kill me." That should work, I thought. But I continued to keep a sharp lookout for taxi drivers on the Inokashira Dōri.

The SPN group went on a last retreat, this time to Kawaguchi-ko, one of the five lakes near Mount Fuji. We stayed in a *ryokan* on a hilltop overlooking the lake and dined around low tables in a big tatami-matted room. After eating my white rice, I held Teddy's infant daughter, Rina, and talked to Aya-*chan*, now missing most of her front teeth. Rory's piercing treble cut through the din. "I don't want Japanese food! I want yogurt!" After dinner we posed for a group photograph. Ikeda must have taken it, because he's not in the picture. Teddy, Sato, Muto, and Ken are holding their children. Dan Uno has his arm around his bride, Sumiyo. In the back row, Spats and Fingers strike poses. The Imp stands with his hand on his hip, spectacles gleaming. Ito-*san*, in a handsome blue plaid shirt, wears a slight, lip-twitching smile.

The lads had planned to play golf or tennis the next morning, but a thin discouraging drizzle was falling from iron-gray skies. A meeting was held to discuss the situation and consensus was eventually reached. We would all head back to Tokyo, but three cars would detour to take a party to Mount Fuji. This party would include the Matsudas and Rhiannon-*san*, who, since they would soon be returning to California, would naturally want to catch one last glimpse of the sacred mountain.*

"One *last* glimpse?" I hissed to Ken. "I haven't had my first glimpse yet! I don't think the damned thing exists. It's a collective hallucination."

"Who do you want to ride with?" Ken asked mildly.

I rode with Stars and Miyuki. The drive seemed to take a very long time. We met the others on a beach. It was cold but it had stopped raining. We walked down to the shore—I kept kick-

---

* Because of SPN's demise, the Matsudas were leaving Japan at the end of November, one year earlier than they'd expected. Dan Uno was leaving early too.

ing stones and yawning—and then we turned around and there, filling the sky, was Fuji-*san*. Snow-capped, it soared out of the flat land around it, perfectly shaped and impossibly high, like a child's drawing of a mountain. Nikos Kazantzakis, I remembered, called Mount Fuji "the heart fo Japan." We stood watching until it disappeared in a shawl of clouds.

A few days before I moved out of my apartment, I threw a party for the SPN group. I should have done this sooner and more often, another lesson learned too late. I made sandwiches and pasta salad. I used the oven to bake two cakes, chocolate-chip and carrot-raisin with cream cheese frosting. I filled my refrigerator with ninety dollars worth of beer, wine, and soft drinks, and exercised my vacuum cleaner.

The apartment looked beautiful. Lamps glowed in every room. Mirrors reflected my collection of Japanese prints. Leafy plants stood about in baskets. A paper doll of a girl in a kimono that Miyuki had given me hung from the white paper lantern in my bedroom. The lacquer basket I'd received at the Ishizumis' wedding was crowded with shiny red apples.

Almost everyone came to my party. Even Ito-*san* came. Christine and Kanji brought their son, Yosuke, and their baby daughter, Tomomi. Muto brought his wife. Miyuki brought a flower arrangement in an elegant black-and-gold lacquer bowl. Ken and Debby brought roses. Rory brought his stuffed lion. (At least he told me it was a lion. The animal had been hugged and cuddled into a shapeless, indeterminate lump.)

The children got passed around like after-dinner mints. I held Rory, Spats held Tomomi, and Yosuke launched himself from Okada's lap into Duncan's while Linette looked on, no doubt thinking that Duncan might as well get into practice. The Imp sat in half-lotus position, talking to Stars and Miyuki. Later, a group posed in the kitchen, Miyuki leaning on the Imp, Teddy leaning on Miyuki, with M.C. smiling in the background. By the end of the evening, after most of the wine and beer had been consumed, SPN members were sprawled all over the apartment. I had to step over them in order to pour tea and coffee.

I didn't have the right temperament to live in Japan. I hadn't learned to read, write, or even speak the language. I don't like raw fish. I can't sit on my legs. I don't have a clue how to culti-vate serenity. I'm not portable at all; I'm incurably Western. But I was surrounded by people I cared about. I had learned all their names. I had taught them some English. I had made them laugh. I had watched one of them cry. In their company I had waded in the Pacific, met a Shinto priest, sung under cherry trees, bowed to the Great Buddha at Kamakura, and traveled to Fuji-*san*. I felt as full as the basket of apples on my coffee table. I wanted the party to last forever.

But the trains stop running at midnight, and everyone had come by train so as to be able to drink. As the Tomodachi got to their feet and went to find their shoes, I passed out my potted plants. They bowed and thanked me for the plants and the party. "*Subarashikatta desu ne!* (It was wonderful!)" Laughing and joking with each other, they made their way into the night. The door closed behind them and I was left with only the things that I could take home with me.

Twenty-Eight

O

"REMEMBER ALL THE BEAUTIFUL TIME."

On my last night in Japan, the SPN group gave a final party for Dan Uno and me. I wasn't on the committee, of course, so I don't know what the code name was. BOW WOW DOG?

I'd been in tears most of the day after reading a spate of farewell e-mail messages at the office. Here is Teddy's:

> Thank you! Rhiannon!
> for writing documentation
> for documentation suggestion
> for English class
> for your kindness
> for your funny's
> and so on . . .
> I hope you to succeed in your novels.
> Best Friendly Regards . . . Iwamoto

It was Halloween, which seemed weirdly appropriate. I'd moved out of my apartment a week earlier. I'd given my bilingual VCR to Yoz and a table and lamp she had admired to

Miyuki. I should have given them proper gifts, not just used stuff. I didn't give anything to Christine, who took me out to lunch and gave me a beautiful white plate shaped like joined-together camellia flowers. We hugged and said goodbye on the train. There were tears in my eyes and, I was amazed to see, in Christine's eyes too. Why hadn't I spent more time with this wonderful person?

Waiting for Miyuki to pick me up in her car and take me to the Matsudas' house, where I was going to stay until I left Japan, I'd walked around my apartment one last time. It was dusty and full of packed boxes. There was a disfiguring stain on the tatami-mat where the air conditioner had leaked. The view from the windows was as ugly as ever. I had loved that apartment. Miyuki had loved it too. She'd stayed in it for several days when I went home for Christmas, getting a taste of independent living. Leaves dropped from the limbs of the huge cherry trees as Miyuki and I drove away from the House of Clear Water.

I was punch-drunk with exhaustion. I fell asleep in the Matsudas' bathtub one evening and Debby had to knock on the door to remind me that I was due at the Marshalls' for dinner. I said goodbye to Mrs. Yamaguchi. She had tears in her eyes too. She begged me to keep up my Japanese and I promised I would. It would be foolish, I thought, to let all that memorization go to waste.

The gifts kept coming. Knowing my fondness for the Annie Hall look, Yoz gave me a tie from Comme Ça Du Monde that had probably cost him a month's salary. Miyuki, who had already given me the beautiful *ikebana* bowl, gave me a cashmere scarf with matching gloves. Her grandmother, whom I'd met only once, gave me an embroidered purse from the poshest shop on the Ginza. I packed these gifts in my big green suitcase and Rory helped me sit on it to get it closed.

On Friday night, Ken and I walked to the restaurant in Kichijoji where my party was being held. It was cold and clear, as Halloween should be. The neon signs looked very bright. I still couldn't read the *kanji*.

I gave my speech. I didn't read it, the way I'd read my speech that night at the Saffron restaurant. After Mrs. Yamaguchi made her corrections, I had committed the speech to memory as a last demonstration of respect and affection for my colleagues.

"*Nihon ni kita toki wa, nihonjin no tomodachi wa zenzen arimasen deshita . . .*" I glanced from face to face as I spoke. Miyuki looked anxious: would I make it through my speech without forgetting anything? Yoz kept stroking his mustache, probably to hide frowns of distress over my pronunciation. Stars and Teddy nodded encouragingly. George stood straight and gazed right into my eyes, as if to lend me strength. The Imp pulled funny faces. Ken smiled all the way through my speech. He was proud of me.

Rory and I would have to open my suitcase again. The SPN members gave me a beautiful round lacquer box, red flowers on a black background, and a photo album. My English students gave me a colorful printed tablecloth. Accompanied by Spats on his guitar, they sang "Do-Re-Mi" from *The Sound of Music*, with lyrics of their own devising.

DO-mo	thank you for this class
RE-member	all the beautiful time
ME-t	with a smile and a heart
FOU-nd	a part of American style
SA-w	a sense of your funny joke
LEAR-nt	a lot of idioms, too
TI-lled	our sense of English use
That will bring us glad to speak!	

Outside the restaurant, to prove that I was still capable of embarrassing the Tomodachi, I hugged them all. Well, not quite all. I wanted to hug Ito-*san*, who had coped so honorably with the strain of working with Westerners, but he looked as if he would run away if I touched him, so I gave him a deep respectful bow.

I sat up late that night, looking through the photo album. Yoz had taken pictures of all the SPN members and Miyuki had arranged them with pictures of Mount Fuji, the *torii* in the sea, "flaming leaves," etc. There was a note from each colleague beside his photo. The managers came first. Ito-*san* hoped that it had been "enjoyable for you to work with us at HPJ." Ikeda appreciated all my help and wished me a happy life in the U.S. Okada wrote, "I never forget to work with you in Ebisu."

They may not have understood my literary ambitions, but the lads expressed confidence in my ultimate success. Sato expected me "to publish sensational fictions in near future," Bobby was looking forward to "your glamorous debut into the literary world" (he has had a long wait, poor lad), and Komori asked for "the right to translate your books." Teddy wrote, "Thank you very much! My English teacher! And let me see your novel."

"You'll be a great novelist," wrote M.C., "I'll be a great comedian." Spats wrote, "I can't forget your waitress at English class." Mr. Goodwrench confided that he was not good at speaking English, "but when I see you next time, I hope I will speak English fluently." His correct use of that adverb warmed my heart.

Muto wrote, "We had a good time with you for job and private time." Stars, depicted with one of his comet photographs, wrote in Japanese but ended in English, "See you again, sometime, somewhere." Fingers had asked to be photographed holding his stuffed animal, a beast unknown to science, a pink blob with a round beribboned head. He promised that he would come to the U.S. next year, "if I win TV quiz."

"Harpo" Sunaga contented himself with printing the conventional phrase, "Please take good care of your health." George wished me good luck. Easy Rider, pictured next to a car rather than a motorcycle, wrote that my English class was very funny. The Imp—a great photo that shows off his customary grin and a single elf-lock of hair curling down his forehead—summed up my feelings exactly: "It's so hard to say Good-by!!"

Everyone thanked me. Yes, *they* thanked *me*. Nagura thanked me "from the bottom of my heart."

Yoz's note was simple. "Hope to see you again always." Miyuki asked me not to forget my Japanese friends. She had arranged the album in four sections, Spring, Summer, Autumn, and Winter. The four seasons are important in Japan. They symbolize the four stages of human life, *shō, rō, byō, shi*: coming into existence, abiding, ending, and returning to emptiness.

Twenty-Nine

THE TOILET-PAPER MAN

Early on the morning of November 1, 1986, Yoz picked me up at the Matsudas' house and drove to the office in Takaido. Half a dozen colleagues had gathered there to follow us to the airport. It was Saturday, the start of a holiday weekend, and pelting with rain. I begged them not to bother, but they insisted. We set out in three cars. Yoz drove me. Easy Rider drove Miyuki (in his car, not on his motorcycle). George drove Teddy, Stars, and the Imp.

Cars on the highway were barely moving. After we'd driven for two hours, I saw a huge street shining with lights. "What's that?" I asked Yoz.

"Ginza *desu*."

"The Ginza? You mean we're still in *Tokyo*?"

The drive should have taken two hours. Instead it took almost four. Yoz tried to distract me by talking and playing jazz, but all I could think about was missing my flight. That and the fact that I badly needed to go to the bathroom.

"One thing I'm not going to miss," I said suddenly. "Several things, in fact."

231

"Tell me."

"The dogs barking all night. The *bōsōzoku* boys. The Buddhist-prayer man."

"The what?"

"The guy in the loudspeaker truck on Sunday mornings."

Yoz looked puzzled. "What does he say?"

I imitated the singsong chant.

"That is *not* a Buddhist prayer," Yoz said. "That is a man who takes your old *news*papers in exchange for *toilet* paper."

"Toilet paper?"

"*Hai.*"

"I didn't learn anything, did I," I said sadly.

"A few, Nano. But a year and a *half* is not enough. For the knowledge to be more *complete*, you must return."

He was right, of course. But I knew that I wouldn't return. Not to live, and perhaps not even to visit. In more ways than miles, Japan was too far from home.

George and his passengers were in the terminal when we arrived, but Easy Rider and Miyuki were still out on the highway. I hadn't said goodbye to them because I assumed I would see them at the airport. I waited for them till the last minute. I waited until George, with his eye on the clock, said, "Rhiannon-*san*, you must go now." Then I hugged everyone, kissed Yoz on the cheek, and walked away as fast as I could, without looking back. There wasn't even time to go to the bathroom before I had to board.

I'd drawn a middle seat between two drowsy men with abnormally sharp elbows. They must have filed them down with sandpaper or something. The smoking section was two aisles ahead of me. For eleven hours I sat as stiff as a *samurai*'s sword, breathing dragon fumes, and waited for the gods to strike. In my lap I clutched my backpack, which contained my novel on diskettes and thirty thousand dollars in traveler's checks. The gods would never let me get away with this. They would not let me have California and money too. Not this much money . . .

The plane slapped down on the runway. "Ladies and gentle-men," said a flight attendant, "welcome to San Francisco."

Ebisu be praised.

Afterword

COMING HOME

It took me weeks to stop saying *"Ohayō gozaimasu"* to my colleagues every morning. I kept chirping *"Dōmo!"* instead of "Thanks," and bowing to bemused Americans. When I entered a shop, I would pause momentarily, waiting for the staff to call *"Irasshaimase!"* I got panic attacks in supermarkets. They were too big, the aisles were too wide, there were too many choices. But there were also sights that moved me to grateful tears. Redwood trees. Mexican restaurants. Bookstores. Naked land with nothing built on it. Every vacant lot was cause for stop-and-stare.

For weeks, when I saw an Asian man from the rear, I would think, "There's Stars" (or the Imp or George or Teddy, depending on who the guy looked like). Then the man would turn and he was just some boring stranger, not the longed-for face with its kind smile or wicked grin. No one talked like Yoz, fast and fluent but with funny emphases. No one spoke as gently as Miyuki. American men were big and clumsy; they loomed over me, and I was not used to being loomed over. American women crossed their legs, wore trousers to work, laughed with their mouths open, and blew their noses in public. Gross.

Worst of all, no one seemed to care that I'd had a profound experience. "How was Japan?" they'd ask, with every sign of expecting an answer in twenty-five words or less. What could I say? "It would take a book to tell you." And they'd edge away, not wanting a book or even a clipped essay. Eventually I worked out the proper response. "It was interesting."

"Cool," they'd respond, and start talking about their deadline or the fact that the big laser printer was down again. Did I look as if I cared?

When Ken and Debby got back to California, we met to compare notes. They agreed with me: culture shock was worse coming home. "We saw some friends over the weekend," Debby told me plaintively. "We'd been in Japan for a year, Rhiannon, but all they wanted to talk about was their weekend at Lake Tahoe."

Like flaming leaves in winter, my good intentions *vis-à-vis* my Japanese friends withered and fell off the tree. I had planned to maintain correspondence with Yoz, Miyuki, Christine, and Mrs. Yamaguchi; to send gifts to everyone; to keep studying Japanese. I kept waiting until there was time to fulfill these obligations properly. I never found the time. It was the same perfectionist, all-or-nothing trait that had doomed my Japanese lessons. I should have gone ahead and done everything improperly.

I did exchange a few e-mail messages with the lads. Teddy and Fingers had been invited to Duncan and Linette's for dinner. The Marshalls' baby was then three months old. "I feel him so heavy," Teddy reported, "but he is standard. I'm surprised with his nose. It's higher than Japanese baby. And his eyes are big and blue." Yoz wrote to tell me that his grandmother, whom I'd met on the Kyūshū trip, had died on March 16. "She met so quiet last life and gone like falling into sleep. She was ninety years old. It's so sad, but dignity."

In February 1987, I used most of my Japanese savings to make a down payment on a Victorian cottage in Healdsburg.

The hunter-green curtains fit my living room windows, and the thousand-dollar Belgian curtains fit my front bedroom windows, without any need for alteration. I've written this book on the desk that Miyuki helped me buy. The Japanese prints hang on my office walls. The Seven Happy Gods look right at home in Healdsburg. By 1990, my house had doubled in value. I wish Matsuda would give me stock tips, but he says my guess is as good as his.

Having a house of my own gave me a boost in confidence. Getting my teeth straightened helped too. Although I complain, of course, about the stresses of self-employment, it suits me. No one minds if I don't start work till noon. There's not a fluorescent tube in sight. The views from my windows are of trees, mostly. Trees and sky. I share the house with the poet Scott Reid.

In September 1988, I finally finished *Terminal Death.* The novel I spent so much of my time in Japan trying to write has never been published. This book, which has been published, could have been even richer if I'd bagged the mystery novel and spent my time taking notes on my Japanese stay. If there is a god of Irony, I'm sure he appreciates that one. He must also appreciate the way I spent eighteen months resisting the Japanese experience and yearning for California, only to spend two years in California trying to recapture Japan on paper.

If there really is a god in everything, then I brought a few gods home with me. On the other hand, if my mother is right about the One True God, then He has been with me all along. And if there are no gods at all and we're on our own, I'm used to that. In any case, most of the time, I'm happy.

But I still have trouble sleeping at night sometimes, and then I think of Tokyo. I miss the Tomodachi. I miss my teacher and her husband. I was never able to tell them how I felt about them all, or to express, adequately, my sense of gratitude. So I wrote this book.

Tsumaranai mono desu ga.